THE PROVEN PATH
TO HOMEOWNERSHIP

YOUR

NEW AND EXPANDED
SECOND EDITION

FIRST

HOME

GARY KELLER AND JAY PAPASAN

Keller
🏠INK

Publisher's Cataloging-In-Publication Data
(Prepared by The Donohue Group, Inc.)

Names: Keller, Gary, 1957- author. | Papasan, Jay, author.
Title: Your first home : the proven path to homeownership / Gary Keller and Jay Papasan.
Description: New and expanded second edition. | Austin, TX : KellerINK, an imprint of Bard Press, [2022] | Previously published: United States : Rellek Publishing Partners, Ltd., [2008]. | Includes index.
Identifiers: ISBN 9781885167934 (paperback) | ISBN 9781885167941 (ebook)
Subjects: LCSH: House buying--United States--Handbooks, manuals, etc. | Mortgage loans--United States--Handbooks, manuals, etc. | Home ownership--United States--Handbooks, manuals, etc. | LCGFT: Handbooks and manuals.
Classification: LCC HD259 .K44 2022 (print) | LCC HD259 (ebook) | DDC 643/.120973--dc23

If you're interested in purchasing bulk copies, please reach out to *Info@BardPress.com*.

Published by KellerINK, Austin, TX; an imprint of Bard Press, Portland, OR.

Paperback: 978-1885167934
Ebook: 978-1885167941

A previous edition of this work was published by Rellek Publishing Partners, Ltd. in the United States in 2008. Second edition published in 2022.

Cover art and layout by Cindy Curtis

Visit *YourFirstHomeBook.com*

CONTENTS

PREFACE

I can still remember buying my first home—it was a big deal. I loved that home, but the funny thing is that it was actually my second choice. I let my first choice slip away. When I found it, instead of buying it, I drove by it every day for almost a week, dreaming about living there. I was certain of my desire to become a homeowner, but I was uncertain of the market and my next move. Unfortunately, on the fifth day I drove by, my first-choice house had a sold sign posted out front. I was heartbroken. But now I knew I couldn't hesitate, and I was certain about what to do next—I immediately bought my second choice.

The reason I share this with you is so you know that even as an experienced real estate agent, I lost the first home I ever wanted. And I don't want the same thing to happen to you. It is also important to keep in mind that your first home probably won't be your last, and making that first purchase paves the way to owning your ultimate dream home faster than you think. As my father, Lew Keller, told me when buying my first home, "Buy it to sell it."

This book is about buying your first home, and I sincerely want to encourage you to make that leap. What's great about owning a home is that it can lay a solid foundation for your financial future while also setting the tone for your personal lifestyle. To be clear, it may quite possibly be the smartest investment you can make.

This book's goal is to be your trusted guide and help you know what to expect. I encourage you to skip around. Dig into the parts that interest you, and skim over those that don't. But first, let me share the most important piece of advice I can give you: You don't need to know everything.

With decades of experience, I've had a hand in thousands of real estate transactions. You know what? I still don't know everything. And I don't want to know everything! Knowing it all, I've found, isn't nearly as important as knowing who you can count on for expert advice. I'm proud to depend on the skills and talents of the people I work with, and that's what I would encourage you to do when you're out there looking for your first home.

Remember, your real estate agent, mortgage lender, and home inspector already know the nuts and bolts. They are market, transaction, and construction experts who will be able to either answer or find the answer to literally any question you may have. And yet, there are going to be some questions that only you can answer: Where do I want to live? What does my ideal home look like? How much can I comfortably afford? Does this home purchase meet my needs and fit my long-term plans?

Real estate agents will tell you that helping first-time home buyers is one of the most satisfying aspects of their work. They know that becoming a homeowner is a huge milestone, and they feel honored to be involved. It's an exciting opportunity, an emotional moment that means many powerful things: You've arrived. You're responsible. You're secure. You're part of a community. You've realized the dream. You're home.

I love what I do and feel honored to be able to help people take ownership of their first home. And, I have no doubt that whoever guides you feels exactly the same. So, good luck on your journey. I hope it's as smooth and enjoyable as it can be, and that you'll be thrilled when you get there—into your first home.

—Gary Keller,
Executive Chairman and
Cofounder, Keller Williams Realty

THERE'S NO PLACE LIKE HOME

Amy and Brian Katz were at a loss. They were sixty days out from renewing the lease on their Nashville, Tennessee, condo when they got a call from their landlord letting them know he was selling the building. At the time, they hadn't had any plans to buy a home. "He offered us the chance to buy it," Amy recalls, "but we decided to look for a house instead." On top of having to search for a new place to live, they were expecting their first child. There was no time to waste. So Amy and Brian set to work. They looked at a dozen houses, but only put an offer on one. It had the most important things they were looking for at the time. Good schools, a great backyard. Plenty of space for their growing family.

In 2013, the Katzes closed on their first home and were elated. They loved that their home had an incredible amount of storage space, including a walk-in attic that they eventually converted into a home office during the COVID-19 pandemic. And on top of that, they also discovered that their first home purchase is now worth quite a bit more than they originally paid. It's turned out to be not only a great home for them—but a great investment, too.

Homeownership is a thrilling prospect and an exciting adventure, and for most of us it can be one of our biggest achievements. Having a place of our very own, somewhere to share with family and friends *is* a real achievement, both personally and financially. But interestingly enough, owning your own place is a relatively new concept. It's true. For most of human history, very few people ever owned much of anything. (Unless you were a king, in which case you got a home *and* a shiny hat.) The concept of your own home, tucked into a cozy suburb, occurred mostly in the United States and the United Kingdom starting in the nineteenth century. Cities like London, New York, and Boston saw rapid population growth with the onset of the Industrial Revolution. With little room to house all the workers, more and more housing developments cropped up on the fringes of towns. Still, for the most part, this suburban sprawl was isolated to major cities only.

It wasn't until the mid-1900s that changes in the United States paved the way for the dream of homeownership. For the first time, large-scale planned communities of affordable houses were created on a massive scale. Think *Leave it to Beaver*-style single-family homes with freshly mowed lawns. One famous example that still remains is Park Forest, Illinois. Located outside of Chicago, Park Forest was built in the 1940s to support the influx of servicemen returning from World War II. Initially, it was comprised of multi-family rental homes, but quickly grew to include single-family starter homes, schools, shops, and community centers. For as little as $9,000, people could put down roots.

Over time, the notion of the white picket fence became an integral part of the American Dream. To this day, many people view owning their own home as not only a rite of passage into adulthood, but a large milestone in their life. And they should! Homeownership provides us with our own safe haven, and it has also become one of the main drivers of generational wealth. But the idea of who owns a home, where they live, and with whom is rapidly evolving. While married couples are still the largest percentage of first-time home buyers, single people are now rapidly becoming homeowners, too. And shortages of single-family starter homes have also led to different patterns in homeownership, with many people opting for condominiums and townhomes instead.

Take Melissa and Kevin Ankin. In 2016, they decided it was time to begin looking for their first home in Kingsland, Georgia. They needed a place that was close to an airport for Kevin's work, required no renovations, and had a backyard for their pup, Bella. After looking at several different properties, they eventually put an offer on a duplex with three bedrooms and two baths for $185,000. "We loved the easy maintenance, access to a pool, and affordable HOA fees," Melissa says. "And the subdivision had a lot of sidewalks, which was very important for our dog."

Over the next several years, they realized just how well the duplex worked for their family. Melissa, whose job was remote, turned one of the bedrooms into an office and could work looking out a large bay window as Bella snoozed comfortably at her feet. Melissa also loved the open floor plan; this meant she could keep a watchful eye on her daughter playing with her stuffed animals while she was in the kitchen. Meanwhile, Kevin loved that he was easily able to fly out of nearby Jacksonville for his job. It was a home that fit both their lifestyle and their needs, even if it was not a traditional stand-alone house.

Now, as their family readies to move into their second home, they've seen firsthand how a home they love can be an investment that grows in value. Their first home went on the market for $249,900—an increase of almost $65,000 in just five years! Buying the right home can truly pay off over time. And many times that can be true even if the home needs improving.

For first-time buyers Becky and Matt Sirpis, relocating to Richmond, Virginia, offered them the opportunity to realize their dream of homeownership and to add their personal touches to the place. They decided on a wonderful 1941 Dutch Colonial home for $350,000 because they loved everything about the house and saw the potential for more. As Becky says, "It was really cute, in a great neighborhood, and it had the indoor and outdoor space we needed."

As much as they loved their house, it wasn't long before they set out to transform it. Becky and Matt turned the first-floor office with paneling and built-ins into an owner's bedroom suite because it already had a full bathroom attached. They also took the kitchen down to the studs and completely renovated it. To give their children a fun space of their own, they turned an area of the basement into their family room. Over the eight years that the family lived there, "We painted every room in the house at some point," Becky says. That vision and hard work helped them remake their home into one that better suited their family, and it added to the value of the property when it eventually came time to move on. They were able to sell the home for $566,000—an appreciation of almost 40 percent!

Your first home may be a duplex or a classic, single-family home. It may come with jewel-toned carpets or solid beige walls. It may be a challenging fixer-upper, a quaint old cottage, or a sleek modern apartment—but from the moment you unpack your furniture and start hanging pictures, your home becomes a mirror that reflects your taste and personality, likes and dislikes, values and dreams. The word "décor" comes from the Latin *decorare*, which means to adorn or embellish. When we decorate our homes, we're adorning them with bits of who we are.

Owning your own home can be a wonderful experience. Through time and attention, you're able to take a relatively blank slate and turn it into something uniquely yours. Your home will ultimately become your haven—a place where you can truly be yourself and escape from the daily grind of the outside world. Once that front door is shut, you are home. Your place. Your space.

There are many firsts in the adventure of life. First day of school. First time behind the wheel. First day at a new job. Saying, "I do." Having a child. Buying your first home. All of these unique moments bring special meaning to your life as you author your own story. Your first home can be the home to many many other firsts. That's why getting it right is so important.

ALTHEA OSBORN'S FIRST HOME

Homes can help us to feel safe and grounded, in spite of what's happening in the world. The house I grew up in, Glazenwood Cottage, was purchased by my grandmother for my mother and located about twenty-six miles south of London. I was a child in England during the Churchill days of WWII, as I like to call them. Despite being in the direct line of air raids, which required us to evacuate for about two months during The Blitz, it always felt safe and comfortable at Glazenwood Cottage. I remember the grand piano my mother would play in the drawing room, the magnolia stellata tree that would turn into an umbrella of flowers in the spring, and the park where my mother and caretaker used to take us for walks. We didn't have much money, so my mother would rent out a room as a first-level apartment to doctors

Photograph of Robert Osborn and son Richard courtesy of the Osborn family.

and nurses who had been evacuated from London to work at our local hospital. My mother cooked breakfast for all of us, including the tenants, and we ate together every morning.

Years later, I met my husband in Germany in 1958, while I was in the British Secret Service and he was in the military. We married a year later. We knew we wanted a home of our own, but the early years of our marriage didn't provide much opportunity as we moved frequently and almost always lived in military quarters. In fact, we moved twenty times during the first eighteen years of our marriage. Finally, we had the opportunity to buy a home in the mid-1960s when we moved to the Washington, D.C., area.

We looked for a house for a month and stayed with friends until we found the right one. The two-story home was at 2849 Maple Lane, on an acre of property off a quiet road in Fairfax, Virginia. Priced at $26,500 and located just six miles from the Pentagon, where my husband was working, the house was ideal for us. It was near schools and in a neighborhood full of children, and it had plenty of space for our children to grow.

During my years as a Realtor, I would tell my clients that if you buy a home when you have children, you're actually buying the place for them. The house on Maple Lane was such a house. My favorite memories of that home are of my children, and I loved being able to provide them with the solid feeling of having a home of their own.

I believe that you become much more rooted when you have a home to call your own. When my husband was stationed in Vietnam during the war, the topic of selling the house came up. We had both left—my husband for the war and myself and the children to live at Glazenwood Cottage with my mother for the year. However, I really felt it was important to have a home to call our own. If something happened to my husband, I wanted to know we had a place to return to that was ours.

We lived at 2849 Maple Lane for three years. We lived in many cities after Washington, D.C., but held onto that first home as a rental, until my husband retired in 1980. When we sold it, it had appreciated to almost $160,000. About ten years ago, we revisited the area and saw it was then valued in the $700,000s. When I think back to what I learned from that house, I'll always recall how owning it rooted us as a family, how it felt like it was ours to make memories in, and how home is always a place where you feel safe from the world.

Althea Osborn joined Keller Williams in 1983 as one of its first agents and has served thousands of clients throughout her career—and she continues to work and connect with many of them today.

CHAPTER 1

DECIDE TO BUY

Dorothy took on a wicked witch, Odysseus fought for ten years, and three brave pets all went on an incredible journey to get to one special place—home. Far from simply being where we live, our home is that happy place where our heart is.

Few things are more exciting than the thought of buying your very first home. But, like learning the really intricate rules of the board game your friend brought to game night, it can also be a tiny bit intimidating. (Seriously, can we just play *Monopoly*?) There's a ton of new terms to learn, professional services you've never used before, a process you're not familiar with, and legal documents that might as well be written in Greek—and you've barely begun!

As you begin your journey to buying your first home, a lot is going to happen. We want you to remember that you will be expertly guided through this process, and, because of this, it will be easier than you think. However, a general understanding of each step along the way will help you be more comfortable and confident. Each chapter of this book will introduce you to the language, concepts, and events you can expect as you move through the ten steps of buying a home.

A Way with Words

As you go through the book, we'll be introducing a lot of different terms, some familiar and some new. Generally, we do our best to define them within the text, but—just in case—we've provided a glossary of terms at the back of this book.

The Ten Steps to Buying a Home

Congratulations! Whether you know it or not, you've already taken the first step on your homeownership journey—you've become interested in buying a home. In this chapter, we'll walk you through the decision to buy and why it's the right choice for you. The next step is to find trusted advisers to guide you through the process. In Chapter 2, we'll discuss how to choose your real estate agent who will educate you about your local market, guide you in your search, negotiate on your behalf, and make sure no critical detail falls through the cracks. Your agent will be your advocate from beginning to end.

The Ten Steps to Buying a Home

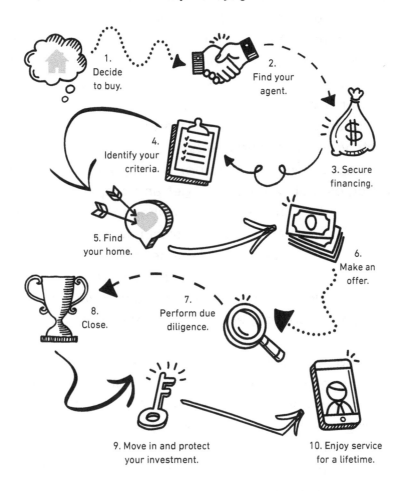

1. Decide to buy.
2. Find your agent.
3. Secure financing.
4. Identify your criteria.
5. Find your home.
6. Make an offer.
7. Perform due diligence.
8. Close.
9. Move in and protect your investment.
10. Enjoy service for a lifetime.

Once you've found your agent, do you know what the next step is? If you said "secure financing," you're right on the money. Chapter 3 explains the factors you should consider as you weigh the many financing options available in today's mortgage market. Then, it's time to start your home search. But what does that even look like? Chapter 4 will prepare you for the questions to ask yourself during this critical stage. Does the house have a moat? Is there a fireman's pole you can slide down from the bedroom to the kitchen? Is there a yard full of chocolate trees? Armed with your *totally reasonable* home-search criteria and a loan preapproval letter, you'll be ready to go find the right home for you, and we'll equip you with proven strategies for your home search. Chapter 5 will give you advice for how you and your agent can get out on the road and find the home that meets your wants and needs.

Chapter 6 will explain offer writing and negotiating strategies that will help you get an accepted contract. However, the game doesn't end when the seller accepts your offer. The period from contract to close is when you and your agent will make all the necessary verifications (due diligence) to assure your home is financially, legally, and structurally sound. Chapters 7 and 8 will walk you through this critical period, guiding you through all the different inspections, qualifications, and steps to take for things to go smoothly. Chapter 9 outlines our tips for moving in and taking good care of your home—as a place to live and as an asset to sell. And, finally, Chapter 10 will give you advice for investing in your home so that it grows in value.

All of this may feel tedious at times, but it will also be totally worth it.

"I remember buying my first home with my wife like it was yesterday!" recalls Jeff Reitzel, real estate broker in Ontario and cofounder of Keller Mortgage Canada. "We were living in a small condo that I had purchased as an investment with my brother before I bought that first house. My wife and I booked a showing to see the home, and when we pulled up, we literally had butter-flies in our stomachs. I fumbled getting into the lockbox, opened the front door, and we both looked at each other and said, 'This is it!'" For the Reitzels, it was not only just the right home, but a warm, loving place to start a family. "Both of our kids were born in that house. Our first home and the experience of buying it are things we will remember forever!"

Making the Call: Am I Ready to Buy?

Buying a home is a big decision—particularly your first home—but it is one of the best choices anyone can make. For starters, having your own home is, well, nice. It's a place that is entirely your own. Something you can paint, renovate, and live a full life in. While renting offers some of these benefits, at the end of the day, the house you rent still isn't *yours*.

Secondly, while they do require an initial investment, the reality is that homes are an incredible way to accumulate generational wealth. Because home isn't only where your heart is, it's where your money is, too. There are few places you will treasure more than your home and no place that will add more to your personal treasury.

Many people don't fully grasp the importance of financial independence or that homes are a great way to realize that goal. Homeownership brings many opportunities—you might say that having a home can open up a lot of doors. For instance, you could later refinance your home to lower your payments or fund home improvements or additions. Or, down the line, you can look forward to the joy of paying your home loan off and reducing your cost of living. This not only feels personally liberating, but it can free up your finances to make other investments. As Tuscaloosa, Alabama, agent

Tricia Gray reiterates, "Most first-time home buyers were previously paying rent, so when they step into home-ownership, they are paying their own mortgage instead of someone else's."

One of the biggest gifts a home gives you is equity.

The Beauty of Building Equity

Net worth, we believe, is one of the best measures of wealth available. **Net worth** is simply the dollar amount you get when you add up everything of value you own and subtract everything you owe. A recent US Federal Reserve Board's Survey of Consumer Finances showed homeowners had a median financial net worth of $255,000, while renters net worth was just $6,300. This disparity is largely due to one thing: equity.

So, what is equity and how does it make homeown-ership a smart financial decision? Equity is the portion of your home's value that you actually own. That is, it's the money that would go into your pocket after you sold it, paid off your mortgage, and handled any selling expenses.

There are two ways to build equity in your home. The first is by paying down your mortgage. Unlike with most purchases, when you buy a property, you're only required to pay part of the sales price up front. This is your **down payment**. For the remainder, you take out a loan that you agree to pay back in monthly installments over a period of years. This loan is called a mortgage loan, which means that you're pledging your home as collateral—that you have, in fact, mortgaged your home. A portion of these monthly mortgage payments applies toward the **principal** (the original amount you borrowed) and the other portion goes toward **interest** (the cost of the loan). Over time, as you pay back the principal, you gradually start to own more and more of the home's value. In other words, you build up equity.

Understanding Equity: Paying Off Your Home

Your first step toward building equity is your down payment. After that, a portion of your monthly payments slowly pay off what you owe toward your mortgage. This means you own more of your home's value. Once you finish paying off your house, you own all of its initial value plus any appreciation.

Closing Day	Year 22	Year 30
Equity buildup begins	Home is half paid off	Home is paid off

Figure 1.1

As Figure 1.1 indicates, many people are surprised that on a thirty-year mortgage it can take as long as twenty-two years to pay off half the principal. This is because early in the life of a mortgage, the majority of your payment goes to interest. You see, the interest you pay on a monthly basis is directly proportionate to the amount of principal you owe at that point. Thus, as your monthly payments reduce your principal, the percentage of your monthly payment that is interest is reduced as well. The net effect is that the closer you get to the end of your loan term, the more principal debt you pay off. (As you'll learn in Chapter 10, if you make one extra mortgage payment a year, you can end up paying off your principal, and thus your loan, much sooner and save money in the process.)

Interest vs. Principal

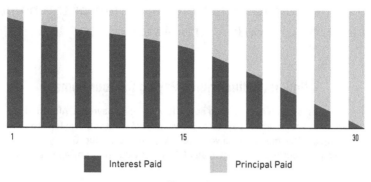

Interest Paid   Principal Paid

Figure 1.2

The second way to build equity is through price **appreciation**. Like most consumer products, homes tend to go up in price over time. A cup of coffee doesn't cost a nickel anymore, and the homes GIs bought in Park Forest back in the 1950s definitely go for more than $9,000. This is a good fact to bear in mind if your current market doesn't appear to be experiencing appreciation. Appreciation is a waiting game—markets always change, and eventually you'll appreciate appreciation. Given time, when you sell your home, we believe there can be an opportunity for you to experience both the bittersweet feeling of moving on and the excitement of making some money on the sale.

With proper planning, your home can become a lot like an interest-bearing savings account. You make regular deposits with each mortgage check you write. Meanwhile, you have the opportunity to earn bonus interest through price appreciation on the value of your home over time. That's a big reason homeowners tend to have a far greater net worth than renters.

Look at the last thirty years. Home values have gone up an average of 3–4 percent annually. Even with events like the Great Recession, there has been a steady increase in home values since the 1970s. While single-digit percentage points might not seem impressive, it would amaze people that just over 4 percent would result in such huge gains—it adds up in a major way. Remember Becky and Matt Sirpis and that 1941 Dutch Colonial that they got for $350,000. A mere eight years later, they sold it for $566,000—that's a remarkable appreciation of 40 percent!

Understanding Equity: Home Appreciation

	Closing Day	Year 22	Year 30
Purchase Price:	$250,000	$250,000	$250,000
Appreciation (4%):	$0	$366,179	$560,849
Current Home Value:	$250,000	$616,179	$810,849
Remaining Debt:	$200,000	$97,855	$0
Total Equity:	**$50,000**	**$518,324**	**$810,849**

Figure 1.3

Figure 1.3 shows an example of the combined advantage of equity buildup and debt paydown. In addition to the two benefits of building equity through mortgage payments and appreciation, there's a third reason why buying a home is financially smart. The United States government allows a **tax deduction** for the interest paid on mortgage loans. We believe the significance of this deduction cannot be overlooked, especially in the first years of a mortgage when interest makes up the bulk of your monthly payments. For example, if your loan payment was exactly the same as your rent, your annual housing costs—including property taxes and insurance—could actually be comparable once you factored in these mortgage interest tax savings. While tax deductions for interest paid are not the same in Canada, homeowners do benefit from not having to pay a **capital gains tax** when they sell their primary residence.

There are solid financial reasons to support your decision to buy a home: equity buildup, value appreciation, and tax savings. But too often people will talk themselves out of making one of the best financial decisions of their lives for reasons that just don't make sense. A lot of this doubtful self-talk comes from one simple thing: fear.

There are a number of fears around trying something new, particularly when that something involves finances. But *fear* not—below we discuss the most common concerns that might keep some first-time home buyers from making the transition from renter to homeowner and the facts to help you make an informed decision.

Those who have the most fulfilling lives base their decisions on facts, not fears.

Fears About Buying Your First Home

1. I can't afford to buy a home now.
2. I should wait until the real estate market gets better.
3. I don't have the money for the down payment.
4. I can't buy a home because my credit score isn't good.
5. I can't afford to buy my dream home.
6. I should wait to buy a home until I'm certain about my domestic future.
7. I should pay off my student loans before buying a home.

Fears and Facts About Buying Your First Home

When it comes to the market, it's reasonable to assume that there is always some measure of uncertainty present. In more recent history, both economic and health-based struggles have added to that uncertainty, making it safe to say the economy and the way we do things—even buy and sell homes—have radically changed. Uncertainty is stressful, and it can be easy to expect the worst.

But that isn't necessarily the case. In fact, you can find a great home in both depressed and elevated markets. Moreover, it's important to remember that market cycles are always occurring. Markets go up and down. The reality is there's never really a perfect market—just the market you're dealing with when you're buying your home. You'll rarely be able to time the market, but if you can afford what you buy and hold onto it long enough, the best timing will find you.

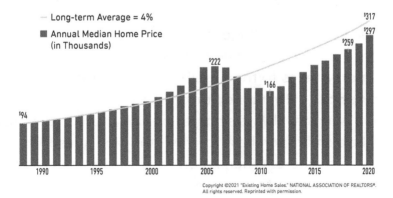

Home Prices (Annual)

— Long-term Average = 4%
■ Annual Median Home Price (in Thousands)

$317
$297
$259
$222
$166
$94

1990 1995 2000 2005 2010 2015 2020

Figure 1.4

Long-term factors make real estate a solid investment. All you need to do now (in the short run) is find a good buy (based on your needs and what is currently available) and make sure you have the financial ability to hold onto it for the long run. Once you've made this purchase, the long-term benefits of equity buildup, value appreciation, and tax benefits will always make it the right decision.

While you should always be aware of the fluctuations of local market conditions, real estate tends to be much more stable and rewarding over time than other types of investments. With the help of your real estate agent, you can find a home that meets your criteria and is a smart purchase.

We hope you're ready to say goodbye to your worries and hello to your good buy. But if you're still feeling anxious about the possibility of buying, here are some great points to consider:

Fear #1: I Can't Afford to Buy a Home Now

Fact: Until You Do the Math, You Don't Know What You Can or Can't Afford

Buying a home is a huge step and a big financial commitment. From down payments to inspections, figuring out **property taxes** to the possibility of **private mortgage insurance (PMI)**, money talk can seem overwhelming. There is almost always a home you can afford to buy that will be a smart purchase for you—the only questions are what and where. When it comes to affordability, there are a few things to consider.

For starters, if you are currently paying rent, generally you can afford to buy. From a financial point of view, in the United States, the tax savings on **mortgage interest** alone usually make up most of the difference between rent and a **mortgage payment**—the tax write-offs you get at the end of the year will generally help you save a significant amount of money.

Understanding the Impact of Interest Deductions

Margot's monthly mortgage payment is $1,208. This means, her payments total $14,496 annually. However, a percentage of that monthly payment is purely interest, which she can write off as a tax deduction in the United States. For instance, in her first year, $11,008 of her annual payment was interest. Depending on where she lives and what tax bracket she's in, Margot could save between $3,000 and $4,000 in taxes, bringing her annual house payments to $10,496–$11,496.

Margot's friend Jacob rents because he doesn't think he can afford to buy just yet. He pays $1,000 in rent per month—that's $12,000 a year in housing expenses. And, unlike Margot, none of it is tax deductible. So, he's paying around $1,000–$2,000 more a year, and he's not even building any equity.

Figure 1.5

Don't believe us? Well, that's fair. We're strangers. But maybe you'll believe *math*. Let's use the example in Figure 1.5: if Margot has a fixed-rate mortgage at 4.1 percent for 30 years and her property will one day be worth $810,849, over the life of her loan she would pay $434,878 in mortgage and interest payments. By comparison, Jacob, over that same 30 years, would have paid over $797,266 in rent assuming his monthly payment increased an average of 5 percent per year. In reality—it would probably be significantly more. In the past 30 years, the cost to rent has risen significantly. One study conducted by the Harvard Joint Center for

Housing Studies found that the "median asking rent for unfurnished units in a new apartment building between July 2018 and July 2019 was $1,620—about 37 percent higher than the median for units completed in 2000." That's a huge jump! The bottom line? After thirty years, Jacob would have spent almost three-quarters of a million dollars, or more, and Margot would have earned more than half a million dollars.

"I knew if I could afford to rent, I could afford to buy," says Donna Corbin, a twenty-one-year-old student in Las Vegas, Nevada, who bought her first home with a government-insured, no down payment program. If you think you can't afford to buy, you might want to ask yourself a different question: "Can I really afford to keep renting?"

Moreover, depending on your credit scores, you can end up affording more than you realize. There are three major credit companies that lenders pull credit scores from: TransUnion, Experian, and Equifax. But the credit scores used for mortgage lending aren't generally the same ones used for, say, your credit cards. Instead, lenders tend to rely on **FICO** 2, 4, and 5—those are mortgage-specific credit scores. (To learn more about credit scores, see Chapter 3. And note that if you're a Canadian resident, you'll rely on what's known as a BEACON score.) These scores tend to take a much larger picture of your overall credit health, considering things like your **debt-to-income ratio**. If you have good credit, you'll get better interest rates on your loan. That could potentially mean buying a house for less money than you'd be paying in rent.

How to Calculate Your Debt-to-Income Ratio

Calculating your debt-to-income ratio is quick and straight-forward. To start, you need to add up all of your monthly debts: credit card bills, student loan payments, car notes, etc. Once you've added all of that up, simply divide that number by your gross monthly income (aka how much money you make before taxes.) For example, let's say you owe $2,500 a month in debt. Your monthly gross income is $5,000 a month. 2,500/5,000 = 0.5. Multiply that number by 100 to get your percentage. In this instance, your debt-to-income ratio is 50 percent. That means half of your gross income is eaten up by debt—that's pretty high. Most lenders are looking for people with a moderate to low debt-to-income ratio for one simple reason: the lower the number, the lower the risk you'll be unable to pay back your loan.

For example, let's say you're presently paying $1,400 in rent per month. You decide you want to buy a home and realize because of your credit score of 740, you'll have a 3.21 percent interest rate on a thirty-year mortgage. Luckily, you've been able to save the past few years and have enough to put 20 percent as a down payment—your monthly payment would be a hundred dollars less a month. Think about that: for less money per month, you could own your own home.

Moreover, homeownership can offer the value of long-term personal and economic stability. Although there may be a higher initial cost to buying a house, if you're planning on staying in one place for a few years, the equity you'll build can end up being a financial boon. The earlier you buy a house, the earlier you benefit from equity buildup. Additionally, you're well positioned for any future appreciation if the market value of the house increases.

For example, if you purchase a home for $300,000, with a 20 percent down payment and covering the remaining $240,000 with a mortgage, you'd have equity of $60,000 in the house. If the market value of the house remains constant over the next two years, and $16,000 of mortgage payments are applied to the principal, you would possess about $76,000 in home equity at the end of the two-year period.

There you have it: the sooner you get into your home, the sooner you'll reap the financial benefits. And the sooner you seriously begin the process of buying your home, the sooner you'll find the home that makes you swoon.

Fear #2: I Should Wait until the Real Estate Market Gets Better

Fact: There Is Never a Wrong Time to Buy the Right Home

Simply focusing on the market is rarely the smart approach to buying the right home. Whether "right" means the right price or the right property for you, waiting for the perfect market timing seldom works to your advantage. Trying to time the market in the short term is the easiest way to miss your timing for the long term.

If you don't believe us, look back at the Great Recession. Starting in 2008, when the bubble around the housing market burst, gross domestic product (GDP) declined by 4.5 percent and unemployment rose to around 9.5 percent. These years had a lasting impact on the economy, culture, and housing market in the United

States. Homes were foreclosed on, new college graduates couldn't find jobs, and retirement funds were drained. Since then, Millennials, in particular, have struggled to make up those gaps, with a mere 47 percent homeownership rate. According to the Housing Finance Policy Center, that puts Millennial homeownership rates for ages 25–34 at 8 percentage points lower than Boomers at that age, and 8.4 percent lower than Gen Xers. Everyone still feels the impact of this incredible financial event.

But, like those who endured the Great Depression, the people who lived through the Great Recession made it through, and benefited from an era of financial growth. In fact, immediately following the Great Recession, the United States entered the longest period of rising prices and general prosperity since World War II. The fact of the matter is, even the biggest economic downturns are, well, normal. They're part of the ups and downs of life. Moreover, they aren't forever. For instance, the Great Recession began in 2007 and ended in 2009—that's only two years! Compare that to the decade-long period of growth and financial stability that's followed. Even when there were some events that threatened to dampen the economy, like the COVID-19 pandemic, the housing market still continued to thrive and interest rates were historically low.

The truth is there are always fluctuations in the market, economic hurdles, and global transformations that impact each generation. While the particularities of those events might change, the overall takeaway is simple: things that go up, eventually go down, and things that go down, eventually go up.

In the end, there are really two ways to make money

in real estate: timing and time. That is, you either happen upon the right moment to purchase your home before its price appreciates, or you hold it for a long enough time so that appreciation makes your purchase investment right. If you miss the first, you most certainly can count on the second.

Fear #3: I Don't Have the Money for the Down Payment

Fact: There Are a Variety of Down-Payment Options Available to You

While many people believe that making a home purchase requires a substantial down payment, as much as 20 percent, this is seldom true. As a first-time buyer, options are always available to you that require much less than this number, as low as 5 percent, some even less. Moreover, most states have down-payment assistance programs that can help you afford to buy. Don't let a lack of a substantial down payment prevent you from investigating your home purchasing opportunities.

House-hacking can also be a great way to make homeownership a more affordable option. House-hacking is when you purchase a piece of real estate—a single-family home or duplex—and lease out one of the bedrooms or units. This rental income can then be applied toward your mortgage. House-hacking is a great way to afford a house that may be otherwise out of your price range or make a mortgage in general more affordable. (We'll cover this more in Chapter 3). Or you can participate in home rental programs like Vrbo or Airbnb. While that might not be ideal all of the time, you could always make your month's mortgage payment by renting out your place while you're on vacation. You deserve time off; let your home make some extra money for you while you rest. The reality is there are many legitimate and sound financing options to choose from, and it only makes sense to investigate which one is right for you, your circumstances, and your pocketbook.

If you're vacillating on whether or not you should spend more time saving up for your down payment or get right down to it, remember that the longer you hesitate, the longer you'll be delaying all the financial benefits of homeownership. In other words, continually putting things off in the hopes of a better market or larger down payment could actually cost you money in the long run.

Fear #4: I Can't Buy a Home Because My Credit Score Isn't Good

Fact: A Less-Than-Perfect Credit Score Won't Necessarily Prevent You from Buying a Home

Typically, there are two main types of credit challenges—a poor credit history or no credit history. Although it's valuable to have a good credit score, a poor one shouldn't necessarily prevent you from talking to lenders to explore your options. You might be pleasantly surprised by the outcome. You can expect that a good loan officer (or mortgage specialist) will be able to help you resolve your credit challenges, often by simply showing you how to move or consolidate your debts, or by referring you to a credit counselor who will put you on a plan. This plan may take a few months or longer to implement, but it immediately gets you on the path to ownership.

If you're facing the challenge of having no credit history because you are new to the workforce or have not made regular purchases on credit, there are still possible solutions that you may want to explore. One common avenue for first-time home buyers is to secure financing with the help of a cosigner, such as a parent or a close relative, who is willing to stand by your ability to make the payments. Another option can be finding a lender who is willing to use alternative forms of payment history such as student loans, rent, and utilities. Some of these may already be creating a credit history, depending on your location and whether or not your landlord has opted in.

It's worth noting that there is no better way to improve or establish your credit rating than by having a mortgage and making timely payments.

Fear #5: I Can't Afford to Buy My Dream Home

Fact: The Best Way to Get Closer to Buying Your Dream Home Is to Buy Your First Home

Very few people can afford to buy their dream home when they buy their first home. In fact, according to the **National Association of Realtors®** (or **NAR**), 78 percent of first-time home buyers in the United States compromised on some features of their first home. This isn't a bad thing! This approach gets you closer to owning your dream home because you are building equity.

Gary Keller and his wife Mary serve as a great example of how this works. They used their first home as a savings plan for their future dream home. They even made additional principal payments when they could to accelerate their equity buildup. This allowed them to pay off their first home in about sixteen years—fourteen years before their original 30-year mortgage would have been paid off with minimum payments. Then, all that financial equity was available to help them build a second home—their dream home.

Fear #6: I Should Wait to Buy a Home until I'm Certain About My Domestic Future

Fact: You Do Not Have to Wait until You're Married, Partnered, or Ready to Have Children to Buy a Home

When most people say they want to wait until they're in a committed relationship to buy their first home, what they're actually struggling with are two distinct issues: First, would it be better to wait until they had two incomes? And, second, will their future partner like their home?

But partnership isn't always something people want, and there's a growing number of singles buying homes too. Putting off the decision to buy the right home is never the best solution. Getting into the game as soon as possible is. In fact, NAR reports that 27 percent of first-time US home buyers are, in fact, single. Of that 27 percent, 17 percent are single women. They didn't wait, so why should you?

If partnership is in your future, then buying is also the right decision. If your future partner doesn't feel at home in the house you've purchased, you can rent it or sell it and use the proceeds, along with your possible dual income, to buy a home you both like. And, if your spouse likes the home you have, then there's no problem at all!

Fear #7: I Should Pay Off My Students Loans Before Buying a Home

Fact: Student Loan Debt Doesn't Prevent You from Buying a Home

Many of us spent a portion of our formative years acquiring wisdom, knowledge, and something else: student loan debt. Now, more than ever, student loans have become a larger burden on first-time home buyers. In fact, according to a study conducted by the Society of Actuaries, "about 31 percent of Millennials report holding student loans, significantly higher than earlier generations." Here in the United States, there are roughly 45 million borrowers with nearly $1.6 trillion worth of student loan debt, with an average debt per person running around $29,000.

That's a lot of debt.

But having student loan debt doesn't need to prevent you from buying a home. Just remember, there are two major ways student loans will impact your mortgage—payment history and debt-to-income ratio.

The payment history for your student loans is like your payment history for anything—if you are late on a payment, your credit will take a hit. If you want to buy a home, it's important to make sure that you aren't late or unable to make debt payments. If you find yourself having difficulty, you can switch your loan repayment plan. Many people can negotiate for an extended payment plan or, if they have federally owned loans, apply for an income-based plan. These options can help your debt payments be lower now, and then they can increase once you've established yourself and start earning more.

Lowering your debt-to-income ratio takes more time. If you find yourself wanting to own a home but need to lower that ratio—make a plan. Contact a financial adviser, set aside money from your paycheck every month that you can use toward an end-of-year extra payment, or increase how much you pay every month to pay off your loans more aggressively.

And remember, no matter what your circumstances, your agent will be thrilled to work with you. From creating online home tours to digital conference calls, real estate companies are working double-time to make sure agents are prepared to provide you with the best service possible.

You Don't Have to Know Everything

You probably never realized you were surrounded by so many real estate "experts" until you decided to buy a home. All of a sudden, your coworker is telling you why **fixed-rate loans** are the only way to go; your great-aunt Martha in Palm Beach, Florida, is sharing her secret tips for finding a hot deal; and your father-in-law is emailing you blurry flip-phone pictures of postings from the real estate section of the *Hometown Chronicle*. Meanwhile, your Internet search engine is bringing up 2,342,209 pages of options, your boss is explaining why you should never buy north of the river, your hairdresser is urging you to never buy south of the river, and you're about ready to jump in the river.

Relax. Even if you can't stop the deluge of contradictory advice and opinions, you don't have to stress out. As an alternative, we offer you our biggest, most important, potentially most-surprising rule for keeping your home-buying stress to a minimum: You don't have to know everything.

Keep It Simple

Keeping things simple starts with separating the things you need to know from those that are strictly optional. The home-buying knowledge you need falls into three categories:

1. Knowledge of the home-buying process itself
2. Knowledge of your local market
3. Knowledge of your personal criteria

Of those three, the only one you absolutely need to master is the last—what you want, what you need, and what you can afford. You need this knowledge to develop a clear vision of the home you're looking for.

Your agent is the one who will fill in any information gaps about the market and the process that you may have. "Buying a home is one of the largest purchases someone will make in their lifetime," says Vermont agent Adam Hergenrother. "While it's an exciting experience, the process can also be daunting for the first-time home buyer. It's a bit of an emotional roller coaster. That's where our team comes in. It is our mission to transform lives through homeownership, and that includes educating our clients about the market and helping them navigate the process, all while enjoying the experience along the way!"

Once you have a solid vision of what you want and an agent to guide you, it's their job to help you narrow the market to those homes that fit your needs. Once you find that special property, the agent will lead the way as your home is researched, assessed, negotiated, contracted, inspected, appraised, surveyed, fixed, financed, insured, and, finally, purchased.

Of course, if you want to delve into the details, by all means, go ahead. We simply encourage you to remember that it's not necessary. It's perfectly reasonable to build a team you trust and let them handle the fuss.

The Four Fundamental Principles of the Real Estate-Buying Process

Now that you've decided to buy, we'd like to give you some advice to keep in mind throughout the home-buying process. We like to call this advice the "Four Fundamental Principles of the Real Estate Buying Process." No matter how much or how little you decide to learn about the details of your transaction, we've found that these four principles apply to nearly any aspect of the process. In our years of experience, we have identified some basic mistakes first-time home buyers are prone to make. Applying these proven principles will help you navigate through them.

The Four Principles of the Buying Process

1. The rules of real estate are always local.
2. The best deals are usually win-win.
3. Price and value are not the same.
4. Choose with your heart and your head.

Principle 1: The Rules of Real Estate Are Always Local

Markets change from year to year and from neighborhood to neighborhood. If you're shopping for a $250,000 home in San Antonio, Texas, you don't need any advice based on what the market was like when your parents bought or what the market is like in Detroit, Michigan, or, in fact, in the $400,000 price range in Windsor, Ontario. As for your brother-in-law's hot advice for scoring a Bay Area bungalow? Let it go. Your cousin's rules of real estate? Plug your ears. Or, at the very least, take them with a grain of salt. You only need to understand what is available for $250,000 in San Antonio right now—nothing more, nothing less.

Similarly, we also encourage skepticism toward the simplistic advice you may have heard, for instance: *always offer below list price or never look above your price range*. Adages and absolutes like these can blind you to the realities of your unique market, a specific property, or your personal needs, and they can keep you from seizing the opportunities before you.

Real estate laws, procedures, and practices are local. They vary significantly from province to province, state to state, and city to city. The way a real estate transaction closing was handled for your brother-in-law in California or your sister in Québec may not be the way it's handled where you're buying your home. One of the key things your real estate agent will do for you is educate you on how real estate transactions are handled in your area and guide you step-by-step through the process.

Principle 2: The Best Deals Are Usually Win-Win

Everything in real estate is negotiable, so don't be afraid to ask for what you really want. Still, negotiations can end when the parties involved don't agree. The solution? Find a win-win outcome that accomplishes what both parties really need. This is why it's important to prepare for any real estate negotiation by deciding where you will and won't be willing to compromise.

Sit down with your agent and figure out what you're willing to live without and what you absolutely need. Going into negotiations ahead of time with some semblance of what you're okay living without can help you mentally prepare for the give-and-take of the process. But, even then, keep in mind that you're working with other people who have their own goals.

In the end, there is always a certain amount of give-and-take. You hold on to those things you really want, and you offer up those things that the other person wants that aren't as important to you. In Chapter 6, we will show you how to craft a competitive offer in which both the buyer's priorities and the seller's needs are met. Where there's a will, there's a way. Trust yourself, trust the process, and trust your agent.

Principle 3: Price and Value Are Not the Same

People make mistakes when they focus on price, not value. This idea applies to far more than just the home you're buying—it's a smart rule of thumb when it comes to most things in life. Being cost conscious is always wise, but being value conscious is even wiser. Price and value normally correlate: you usually get what you pay for. But when considering a purchase, it's important to go beyond the surface, really think about what it is you want and why, and then expect to pay a fair price for it. And remember: just because something is costly doesn't make it the best, and, likewise, just because it's cheap doesn't make it a bargain.

Just ask Missouri agent Jen Davis. "First-time home buyers have the ability to make a huge financial impact on their future. We need to make sure, as their **fiduciary**, that we guide them to select a home that will hold its value in tomorrow's market. We do this by guiding them to purchase a home that could be used as a rental when they move out or is such a desirable home that it will always be easy to sell. The factors that make that home desirable are price, condition, and location. If we are at or under market averages, we will always be able to compete in any market."

In essence, what you're looking for is a home that will appreciate in value with a few improvements—not a move-in-ready, HGTV home. It's also important to check and make sure there isn't some factor that will cause the house to be ruled out by 50 percent of people right away. Is the house near the airport or an incredibly busy road? Do powerlines run through the backyard? Does the backyard sit next to train tracks? Is it absolutely, 100 percent, definitely haunted? If the answer is yes to any of these questions, then that house may be a poor investment.

As always, it's important to do your research, consider all options, and look for the best overall value—the best quality at a reasonable price. You wouldn't buy a car without doing your homework on make, model, and quality or without considering which car best fits your needs. When it comes to buying your home, it's important to think the same way.

When you purchase your first home, you're more than likely making one of the biggest purchases of your life. This is no time to cut corners. That half-price inspector may save you $200 today, but they could miss a structural problem that might cost you thousands tomorrow. You should be able to count on your lender to lock in the best rate and deliver all necessary paperwork by closing. If a discount lender drops the ball, your closing could be delayed, it could cost you considerably more money, or it might possibly even cause you to lose the home.

So, don't set yourself up for hassles, headaches, or dead deals. Look for value—integrity, reliability, and impeccable service—from all the professionals you hire.

Principle 4: Choose with Your Heart and Your Head

Whatever property you buy will be both your home and a major financial investment. So, you want to find a home you absolutely love—a home that fits your life, located in the right neighborhood. And, at the same time, you want the property to be a solid financial asset—one that is structurally sound and appears to be well positioned to appreciate in the future. In the end, finding that perfect place for you means balancing emotion and rationality. When you're out looking for your future home, go ahead, let your heart guide you. But, when it's time to buy, step back and think with a cool head. In a few years, when you may want to sell the house, you will be very glad you did.

There's No Place Like *Your* Home

Finding a home isn't quite as easy as clicking your heels three times—but it doesn't have to resemble a battle with wicked witches and flying monkeys either. It should be an exciting adventure. With a trusted team of advisers and a handful of clear strategies, you'll have the knowledge and confidence to find the home that's right for you. And then, someday soon, you'll be there. You'll unpack the boxes, pick out draperies, toy with furniture arrangements, and send photos to friends. You'll feel that same satisfaction and excitement that Dorothy felt when she came back from Oz: *there really is no place like home.*

Notes to Take Home

- Purchasing your own home is a great investment.

- Done right, homeownership lays the foundation for a life of financial security and personal choice.

- There are specific financial reasons to buy a home. Among these are equity buildup, value appreciation, and tax benefits.

- It's smart to base decisions on facts, not fears.

- The following facts help dispel fears about purchasing your first home:

  - If you are paying rent, you very likely can afford to buy.

  - There is never a wrong time to buy the right home. All you need to do in the short run is find a good buy and make sure you have the financial ability to hold it for the long run.

  - The lack of a substantial down payment doesn't prevent you from making your first home purchase.

  - A less-than-perfect credit score won't necessarily stop you from buying a home.

  - The best way to get closer to buying your ultimate dream home is to buy your first home now.

  - Buying a home doesn't have to be complicated— there are many professionals who will help you along the way.

  - Student loan debt doesn't have to be a barrier to homeownership.

  - You don't have to know everything.

BILL SOTEROFF'S FIRST HOME

Our homes are the center of our universe. My parents only owned two homes their entire lives. We affectionately called these houses "the old home" and "the new home," even though one was sold for the other decades ago. Although they weren't big homes, I remember the old home being so much bigger than it actually was, because it fit so many people, events, and memories.

My childhood memories revolve around that home. Its garage was in the back of the house, and while the cars got bigger during this time, the garage stayed the same size. There were several times when my mother drove into the garage, wiping it out. My father would just shake his head, call the carpenter, and rebuild it. I remember our neighborhood being filled with children to play with, whether it be hockey in the street during

Photograph courtesy of the Soteroff family.

the wintertime or baseball and basketball in the summer. Once the sun would set and the streetlights would come on, our home would be filled with the neighborhood kids. My mother never turned anyone away.

When my wife, Elisabeth, and I got married in 1980, the dream of homeownership was very important to us. We knew we wanted to have a family, but the apartment we were living in would not be big enough for us. However, we couldn't afford a house. So, I switched jobs, we started saving our money, and we began looking in suburbs outside Toronto for a place to call our own.

We knew the ranch-style home on a dead-end street was the right house the second we laid eyes on it. Although it was a long commute for me to get into the city, 240 Thomas Court fit all our needs and wants. It had a huge, fenced-in backyard that would be great for our future children, it was close to several parks, schools were nearby, and it felt very safe. When we made the $30,000 down payment toward the $80,000 purchase price, we knew it was another step in our lives toward our dream.

Elisabeth and I were so proud of owning that home. When we moved in, we were at the beginning of our life together. We learned how to paint, wallpaper, and fix whatever broke. I remember going to sleep at night listening to the sound of the sewing machine, as Elisabeth made our curtains. We made it our place, and it reflected all of our hopes.

When I think about the lessons I've learned from homeownership, I recognize how important it was for my wife and I to set goals. Every house we lived in over the years was a target we set and worked toward together.

We worked hard to achieve the milestone of our first home purchase. When Elisabeth and I wanted to grow our family, we set our sights on the future. Four years later, we were able to sell our first home for $150,000 and purchase a home that better suited our needs.

Despite living in five different countries and seven different houses over the years, each house became the center of our universe and the setting for so many family memories. There is no doubt that owning a home is one piece of the fairytale for me. With a nice place to call our own, a wonderful wife, and a beautiful family, the dreams I had for my life have all come true.

Bill Soteroff is the president of Keller Williams Worldwide.

CHAPTER 2

FIND YOUR AGENT

For most of early human history, generally speaking, if someone wanted a parcel of land that was already occupied by someone else, they had to fight for it. That's how King William came to own all of England in 1066: he conquered it, declared it his own, and, *voilá*, it was his. In fact, trial by combat was at one point an incredibly common way for people to solve disputes, win legal arguments, and even lay claim to a plot of land. In England, for instance, the feudal system meant that land was owned by the monarch first and foremost. From there, the ruler could give parcels of land to lords, who could then turn around and give parcels of land to their knights or other humbler humans. If lands were ever disputed, lords could challenge one another to trial by combat, with the winner taking control of the property. (And you thought competing with multiple offers was stressful!)

Of course, this was not particularly fair for the vast majority of people involved. Moreover, with the growth of the middle class in Europe and the Americas, the notion of owning property began to spread as feudalism began to fade. So, over the years in many parts of the world, a more equitable system developed where willing parties bought, traded, or sold property.

The Real Estate Agent: a Profession Is Born

These trends from Europe traveled with early colonists and through imperialist practices across the Americas. Small settlements became colonies that then expanded, creating infrastructure that increased trade, and small towns grew into increasingly larger cities. By the late 1800s, with this increase in growth and westward expansion, the laws and transactions surrounding the ways people purchased properties in the United States had become complicated, and real estate specialists emerged. Thus, a profession was born.

In 1908, real estate professionals from around the United States convened in Chicago to form the National Association of Realtors (NAR). This group soon began laying the groundwork for the way buyers and sellers in America do business together today. They began standardizing contracts, creating open and clear procedures, guaranteeing accurate and timely property information, and formulating real estate licensing requirements and a code of ethics.

About the time this was happening in the United States, a similar development was underway in Canada.

In the 1880s, specialists on the west coast set up the first real estate board in Vancouver. Later, real estate professionals established boards throughout the country to address business ethics and industry standards and to encourage a spirit of professional cooperation. From Vancouver to Toronto, organized efforts across the nation culminated in the formation of CAREB the Canadian Association of Real Estate Boards. CAREB soon implemented the "Realtor" designation for its members, and eventually the **Canadian Real Estate Association (CREA)** was formalized with its headquarters in Ottawa.

The legal, financing, and regulatory aspects of real estate transactions have become considerably more involved in order to provide as much protection as possible for both buyer and seller. From the required **contractual disclosures** and **contractual addendums** to the procedures for determining clear **title to property** to the federally enforced regulations (such as the **Fair Housing Act**, the **Americans with Disabilities Act**, and the **Truth in Lending Act**), buyers, sellers, and the professionals who work with them are held to ever-higher standards.

Today, you can expect your agent to advocate for you and your interests throughout the home-buying process. Their job is about much more than simply finding you the right home; it's about listening to your needs, anticipating problems, and maintaining standards. In fact, it's the responsibilities your real estate agent must undertake before and after the home-showing phase that makes having a real estate agent so invaluable. As Nashville, Tennessee, agent David Huffaker puts it, "Trust the agent to guide you through—from contractors to inspectors—they are the key to a smoother, stress-free transaction."

From helping you find the right inspector to sending you your first housewarming gift, good agents should provide you with everything you could possibly need.

"I think first-time home buyers are more confused than afraid. A lot of them know about different parts of buying a home but don't exactly understand how all the parts fit together. Many have done research and know bits and pieces, but not everything," notes Austin, Texas, agent Wendy Papasan. At the end of the day, it's your agent's job to work as your advocate and guide, helping to ease your home-buying experience. They should show you the ropes of homeownership and educate you on the buying and selling process as you go.

The way each agent conducts business may differ in some ways, but, no matter what, there are certain qualities that all top-notch agents have in common. After years of research and interviews, we have found seven distinct and critical responsibilities your agent will fulfill on your behalf.

The Seven Main Duties of Your Real Estate Agent

First and foremost, your agent will serve as your market consultant. You will depend on your agent to educate you about your local real estate market and make sure you understand everything you need to know about the home-buying process in the area where you are looking to buy. When it comes to picking the right agent, we recommend you look for one who listens and then clearly communicates information in a way that makes sense to you. If they can't make what you hear clear, steer clear!

The Seven Duties of Your Real Estate Agent

Your agent will help you in all kinds of ways, but their core duties are to

1. Educate you about your market.

2. Analyze your wants and needs.

3. Guide you to homes that fit your criteria.

4. Coordinate the work of other needed professionals.

5. Negotiate on your behalf.

6. Check and double-check paperwork and deadlines.

7. Solve any problems that may arise.

When working with first-time home buyers, Washington, D.C., agent Kymber Lovett-Menkiti finds it important to establish herself as a partner in her client's journey. "I take the time to sit down with my clients at the beginning of the process, to explain the complexities and the multiple players involved—from mortgage to insurance to inspectors to appraisers to title. I want them to understand the process and ensure they know that I am with them every step of the way. I also find a key aspect of the process to include a genuine conversation regarding needs versus wants. We want to identify a home that fulfills their dreams but also fits their lifestyle—the most they want and can have for the value they can spend."

After orienting you to the market, your agent will help you analyze your needs and wants—including things you may never have considered. Saratoga Springs, New York, agent Christine Marchesiello points out, first-time home buyers often aren't sure what it is they are even looking for. "It's hard to know what your needs will be or what you will ultimately like or want in a home if you've never lived in your own home before." Once your agent has discussed the basics of what to look for in a home and considered your individual needs, they'll guide you through a home-to-home search for a property that meets all your needs and as many of your wants as possible.

Finding that right property can be a challenge! But a good agent will know the area and the market, and they will help you find and secure that perfect home. "Our job is to educate buyers and then help them get into the home and neighborhood that *they* want to live in," says agent Charlotte Savoy of Ellicott City, Maryland. "Some agents think their job is to get their clients the very best deal possible. I believe it's actually my job to help them do whatever it takes to get the house they really want. Our market is competitive, and I don't want anyone to miss out on a house they absolutely love because I didn't do my part to help them win in that competition."

Your agent isn't the only expert whose assistance you'll need throughout the home-buying process. As you move ahead, other specialized advisers, such as a **mortgage officer** and **property inspector**, will also help you complete your purchase. It's important to make sure you look for an agent who can expertly coordinate all the professionals involved in your home purchase. As you're choosing an agent, talk to people who have worked with your agent before, get recommendations or referrals, and talk to other members of their team. You want to make sure they're ready and able to keep all the pieces moving forward.

Your Agent's Team

Your agent is the head of a large team, coordinating a group of professionals who will help you along your journey to home-ownership. Some of those key players in the purchase will be—

- Your agent
- Your seller's agent
- Lender (mortgage broker in Canada)
- Appraiser
- Inspector
- Contractor
- Closing coordinator
- Escrow officer

To help you keep track of the people your agent has working on your behalf, you can check out page 250 and add the contact information for your home-buying team.

In addition to being a skilled project manager, your agent is also your negotiator. This responsibility kicks in from the moment you make an offer on a home, and it doesn't end until you've taken ownership of your home and everything is settled. As an adept negotiator, your agent will always represent your interests and push hard for the best deal. "Every market is different. What to expect when you make an offer can vary greatly from price point to price point and from city to city. Rely on your Realtor to [help you] make a great decision," says Wendy Papasan. If things do get tense, your agent will serve as a buffer between you and the seller or the seller's agent, remaining coolheaded and logical while exploring different options to find a win-win solution. More often than you would think, your agent will actually continue to advocate for you well beyond the closing of the home, helping you tackle the upkeep and responsibilities that can occur after you've taken ownership.

Throughout the closing process, a myriad of details will be resolved behind the scenes. But the good news is that your agent will constantly check to see that timelines are met, paperwork is completed, updates have been filed, and the important steps are completed. Almost without fail, there will be problems. Your agent will prevent them when they can be anticipated and solve them when they are unforeseen. In short, your real estate agent will wear many hats.

You may find your agent through a strong referral from a trusted friend, relative, or colleague, or by your own research. No matter how you first meet your agent, it will benefit you both if you ask a few important questions.

Eight Important Questions to Ask Your Agent

Qualifications are important. However, finding a solid, professional agent means getting beyond the résumé and into what makes an agent effective. Use the following questions as your starting point:

1. Why did you become a real estate agent?

2. Why should I work with you?

3. What do you do better than other real estate agents?

4. What process will you use to help me find the right home for my particular wants and needs?

5. What are the most common things that go wrong in a transaction, and how would you handle them?

6. What are some of the mistakes that you think people make when buying their first home?

7. What other professionals may we work with, and what are their roles?

8. Can you provide me with references or testimonials from past clients?

Professionalism: The Quality That Matters Above All Else

With the right service provider, you should feel safe and secure. The right real estate agent for you understands this and sees service as both a promise to you and a duty to the profession. They will put your interests first, not just because it's a professional duty, but also because it is the right way to treat people. And cordiality is also good business. Successful agents enjoy the long-term benefits of providing stellar service through testimonials and word-of-mouth referrals.

At the end of the day, a good agent will want to build a solid relationship with you—irrespective of whether you want to buy a house right now or not.

"Several years ago, I had the pleasure of becoming friends with a wonderful family. I have stayed in contact with them personally and advised them professionally in real estate whenever I could help. Recently, one of their daughters got engaged. While they weren't ready to put down roots yet, we kept in touch," says Kernersville, North Carolina, agent Amy Cromer. And she did, checking in on the family for several months. Sure enough, two months later, the family contacted Amy again, ready to find the perfect home.

"Our relationships in life are never about business; they are about people first. If you care about people first, they trust you for business later."

Good Agents Put Their Clients First, Their Paychecks Second

Phoenix, Arizona, agent Elaine Sans Souci once worked with a buyer who had been disabled in an accident. It severely limited the woman's memory, and she survived on a disability payment that barely covered her monthly costs.

"She was in the sort of situation where she could do laundry once a month, because she had exactly $1.25 budgeted for laundry," Elaine explains. "When I met her, the mortgage company said, 'Run.'"

But Elaine didn't run. She spent months helping the client get her finances in shape and looking for a home that would save her money. Finally, when she got a property under contract, the client suddenly remembered some recurring costs she had forgotten to tell her lender. With that new information, Elaine realized that there was no way the woman would be able to keep up with the payments. She convinced her client to drop out of the deal.

"Sure, it's hard to walk away from a commission," she says. "But you can't just watch a client get into a situation where you know she'll go down the tubes."

But this story has a happy ending: Elaine eventually found a home her client could afford. This kind of focus, where your agent acts as a true fiduciary and puts your needs above all else, is the gift a good agent will give you. Your partnership with your agent will not only serve you during your home search but hopefully long after.

Know What to Expect

We've all experienced situations where we felt like someone wasn't really listening to what we were saying. You can probably think of one right now—a time when you talked with a salesperson in a store or called your bank or telephone company service representative, and the person (or robot) didn't get what you were asking. In fact, the representative didn't seem to be listening, and their service fell far short of your expectations. Research shows that as consumers we value those professionals who listen carefully and are able to meet or exceed our expectations. A good agent will do just that.

When you have an agent who truly listens to you, a cooperative dialogue develops born of mutual respect. Good agents will explain exactly what will happen during the home-buying process. This is also your opportunity to be very detailed and clear about mutual expectations—ask how often you'll be in contact, how often you can expect to see homes, and how many properties you might visit in an afternoon. Ask your agent how they'll communicate with you, whether by phone, text, or email, and make sure you share your preferences. Ask if other people will be helping your agent and if they'll be contacting you, so that you're not surprised when they do.

When you find the right agent, you will actually be making a mutual commitment. Your new agent will be dedicated to answering all your questions and getting you what you want. You will be committing to honestly sharing your feelings, opinions, and concerns. And you will be committing to work exclusively with that person as your agent. This is usually done formally through a **buyer representation agreement**. When an agent asks you to sign this agreement and you concur, you both agree that, for a set period of time, you will expect only this agent to work in your best interests to find homes that fit your criteria.

The Buyer Representation Agreement

Any strong relationship is built on respect for each party's needs, expectations, and time. That's why many agents like to set mutual expectations with a buyer representation agreement. This document states that any home you buy, you will buy with the help of your agent for the duration of the agreement. It will also explain how the agents involved will get paid. Such agreements can usually be terminated with a couple of days' notice; although, you usually can't terminate the agreement and then go buy a house that your agent previously showed you.

A representation agreement can help you because it gives the agent the confidence that the time devoted to your home search will not go unrewarded, which in turn gives you the agent's very focused attention. These agreements are also useful because they spell out the precise duties you can expect your agent to fulfill, so if they are not carried out, you can point to the agreement and request an explanation. All in all, a buyer representation agreement is a mutual written commitment that clarifies the working relationship.

It's a true win-win.

We truly believe it's important to find the right real estate agent for you, a key piece on your home-buying journey. Finding the right agent isn't complicated, but it will require effort and diligence on your part—it's simply the best way to get your home search off on the right foot. Knowing you've put in due diligence to find an agent you like and trust—someone who can put themselves in your shoes—will help you feel more confident and prepared for the journey to come. The time it takes you to find and select your agent will leave you more educated about the home-buying process, wiser to your local market, and ready to take the next step. That step is usually choosing a reliable lender and getting preapproved for a mortgage that best fits your needs, whether you're well-heeled, on a shoestring budget, or somewhere in between.

Notes to Take Home

- When looking for an agent, know that above all else good agents put their clients first.

- Your real estate agent will perform seven main duties:

  1. Educate you about your market.

  2. Analyze your wants and needs.

  3. Guide you to homes that fit your criteria.

  4. Coordinate the work of other needed professionals.

  5. Negotiate on your behalf.

  6. Check and double-check paperwork and deadlines.

  7. Solve any problems that may arise.

- The buyer representation agreement clarifies the working relationship between the buyer and the real estate agent. It involves making a mutual written commitment—your agent commits to getting you what you want, and you commit to working exclusively with your agent.

DAVE JENKS' FIRST HOME

When we moved to East Lansing, Michigan, my wife, Sherry Dawn, was pregnant with our first child. Twenty-seven months later we had three children—two of our own and a young girl we adopted. It was 1969, and my wife and I were living in a residence hall on the campus of Michigan State University while I worked toward a doctorate in counseling psychology. I was the residence hall director. Three young children and a hundred babysitters—what's not to like?

The students adored our kids, but there was no privacy for a young family, nor enough space. It was clear that there was no way we could live in a student residence hall with three children.

In looking for our first home, we were purely practical. My wife and I both were from rural areas in New York state and were familiar with simple country living. We needed a home we could afford. We found one—a small, two-bedroom, one-story house in an older neighborhood with lawns and trees—and bought it with a no-money-down Federal Housing Administration (FHA) loan. When we shut the door to our new home, we enjoyed complete privacy together for the first time in our lives.

It turned out to be a wonderful, cozy home for a beginning family. The house was probably twenty-five to thirty years old and needed some fixing up. I bought a Time Life book on home remodeling and repair and enlisted a friend who knew something about wiring. We plunged in, building out the attic and adding two more bedrooms, among other improvements.

I knew that I was in way over my head. But it was a lot of fun rehabbing my own home and creating a room for each of our children with my own hands.

As amateur as my work was, it was good enough. We purchased the house for around $30,000. Eighteen months later, I took a full-time job at my alma mater in Albany, New York, and we sold it for a profit.

I learned so much from that experience. My adolescence had been extended because, as a college student and staff member, I had spent years living in fraternity houses and dormitories on several campuses. Buying that home was my first step to serious adulthood. Looking back, I see now that the home was very much like the one I grew up in—down to the refinished walk-in attic.

I believe, in a way, I was following in my dad's footsteps—buying a house and, through my own labor, making it into a home for my family that we could be proud of. We loved our time there—eating dinner together, playing catch on the lawn, and visiting with neighbors. I finally felt like a dad and a grown-up.

Dave Jenks was a coauthor of the first edition of Your First Home *and served as vice president of research and development at Keller Williams Realty.*

CHAPTER 3

SECURE FINANCING

Teresa Van Horn of Madison, Wisconsin, never thought she'd qualify for a mortgage. After getting married at an early age to, as she put it, a "financially challenged" individual—she found herself broke, divorced, and drowning in debt, all before her twenty-fifth birthday. Although she was able to move in with her parents and sort things out, she did pay some bills late and came close to defaulting on her student loans more than once. She thought her credit was ruined forever.

Less than five years later, Teresa had a steady job and a stable income and was regularly paying off her debts. She was ready to stop renting, but one obstacle stood in the way: her credit report. "It took a long time for me to get up the guts to talk to lenders," she says. "I thought they would laugh at me."

They didn't—in fact, Teresa was pleasantly surprised

to learn she qualified for a modest loan.

Although virtually everyone finds the thought of owning their first home exciting, taking out a mortgage can be a daunting prospect. Many first-time buyers, like Teresa, start the process confused or nervous about making such a large financial commitment. A mortgage is a serious responsibility that warrants very careful consideration, but it is also a tremendous privilege. If you couldn't borrow the money to buy your home, you'd have to pay cash. Just imagine what it would be like trying to save the whole purchase price!

In general, you'll probably discover that mortgage loans are less confusing than you might think. Actually, the loan choices out there are all just simple variations on a few major types. In this chapter, we'll walk you through the basics: what a mortgage loan is, how to find a lender, what factors to consider when picking how to fund your mortgage—be it creative or traditional financing—and much more. We'll give you the tools you need to go into any mortgage discussion with a clear understanding of your needs. You can take that to the bank.

So, What *Is* a Mortgage?

In its most basic sense, a mortgage is a loan secured for real estate property. With a mortgage loan, the lender will hold legal title until the loan is paid. The word "mortgage" comes from the French word for "death pledge" because the pledge "dies" when the loan is repaid or the lender forecloses for lack of payment. As a buyer, you can obtain your mortgage loan from a mortgage banker, mortgage broker, savings and loan, credit union, or bank. Beyond the traditional mortgage industry, you may be able to obtain some or all of the financing from private individuals, including the seller of the property. Funding from these private sources is often called "creative financing," which we'll touch on later in this chapter.

"I make sure that the person can get financing before we do the offer," notes Jeff Reitzel. "I don't care about the deal per se, or the seller, if I'm working for a buyer. I've always cared about the buyer. How emotional would it be to have an offer accepted—and you think you're moving into the home with your family—and then have it fall apart because you can't get financing? It would be devastating."

But before you get to touring homes and making offers and all that, you need to know who you're going to get your mortgage from and what types of mortgages are available.

Mortgages: The Basics

Mortgage loans now come in more varieties than ever. But don't let all the different options confuse you. The differences between each type of mortgage loan boil down to four basic factors:

1. Down payment
2. Interest rate
3. Term
4. Fixed vs. adjustable rate

Down Payment

A down payment is the initial payment you make toward your home. It's calculated as a percentage of the entire cost of the house. Historically, home buyers have been asked to put 20 percent down.

So, if you were going to buy a home that cost $200,000 and needed to put up a traditional down payment, you'd need to come up with $40,000. But don't let that big number scare you. These days, buyers can get into properties by putting a much lower percentage down. In fact, there are a number of programs designed specifically for first-time home buyers that allow borrowers to put down as little as 3 to 5 percent toward a new house.

While taking advantage of these new, lower down payments can be a great option for many new buyers, that 20 percent mark has its advantages, too. For one thing, we believe it usually gets you the best interest rate. Generally speaking, the more you initially put down on your home, the better interest rates you can get. Plus, the more you put down, the less you have to borrow—that means a lower monthly payment, as well as paying less interest over the life of the loan. Putting 20 percent down also frees you from **private mortgage insurance**, or **PMI**, in the United States and Canada, which lenders require of buyers who borrow a higher percentage. In Canada, mortgage loan insurance is mandatory for any loan with a down payment falling between 5 and 19 percent. There are three primary providers in Canada: Canada Mortgage and Housing Corporation (CMHC), Genworth Financial, and Canada Guaranty. In the United States, borrowers have to pay a monthly PMI fee, but in Canada a borrower's mortgage loan insurance is actually added to the principal loan amount.

A PMI is basically just a lender protection fee designed to protect lenders against loss if a borrower defaults on a low down payment loan. While it does increase your monthly payment (and it isn't tax deductible), it can be good for a borrower with less cash to put toward a down payment. And, after a few years, when you achieve that 20 percent equity mark in your home through a combination of your original down payment and your monthly payments toward the principal, you'll be eligible to have the PMI policy canceled. Many homeowners don't know this and continue to pay PMI needlessly. Just make certain to keep track of your PMI and take the initiative to have it canceled when your equity gets to 20 percent. While most conventional mortgages will automatically terminate your PMI once you reach 22 percent, it's smart to keep track of it yourself and get out of your PMI as quickly as possible. Remember, there are two paths to 20 percent. You can pay down the debt, and your home can appreciate in value. We'll cover the best home improvements to increase value in a later chapter.

Without a doubt, paying 20 percent down on a home is a sound financial decision. Having a large equity position in your home from day one protects you from unforeseen shifts in the real estate market and lays a solid financial foundation for your future. If you elect another option, we encourage you to consider making additional investments in your home to increase its value or pay down the debt so you can avoid PMI and lower your monthly costs.

Interest Rate

Understanding and securing the best interest rates is an incredibly important part of the loan process. An interest rate is a fee or amount charged by a lender and is usually a percentage of the loan amount. Interest rates are implemented when we buy cars or use credit for a purchase. And, like credit card rates, home loan interest rates are variable—they change with the market. For instance, in the 1970s and 1980s, interest rates for mortgages could be as high as 15 percent. But, for the past decade, most interest rates have been lower than 10 percent. In 2020, interest rates even reached historic lows—under 3 percent!

In general, people want the lowest interest rate possible because that means they're paying less money in interest over the life of the loan. In addition to saving you thousands in the long term, a lower rate will also reduce the amount you pay each month. The example in Figure 3.1 shows that for a monthly payment of $1,200, a 4 percent interest rate on a loan would allow you to buy a home that's worth $100,000 more than the home you could get with an 8 percent interest rate.

Interest Rates Impact How Much House You Can Afford

If you can afford a $1,200 monthly mortgage payment (not including taxes and insurance), a low interest rate can allow you to afford a higher-priced home. Your rate will also determine how much interest you pay over the life of your loan.

Loan Amount	Interest Rate	Monthly P&I Payment	Total Interest Paid Over 30 Years
$150,000	8%	$1,200	$282,000
$200,000	6%	$1,200	$232,000
$250,000	4%	$1,200	$182,000

Figure 3.1

Sometimes people put off buying a home thinking that the market or interest rate will go down. We encourage you to move forward with the purchase of your first home regardless of the current market. For one thing, it's possible that rates will rise rather than drop and that golden opportunity you were waiting for will pass you by. Moreover, if rates improve, depending on your situation, refinancing your home could get you a better rate later on. For example, following the high mortgage interest rates in the 1980s (12 to 18 percent), there was a period of massive mortgage refinancing when those rates dropped below 8 percent in the 1990s.

Refinancing Considerations

Over time, as your home increases in value (appreciation), the amount you have borrowed (principal) will steadily become a smaller and smaller percentage of the home's actual worth.

If you decide to refinance, the new lender will calculate your new loan amount against the new appraised value of your home. Therefore, your loan-to-value ratio (LTV) could now be at or below the 80 percent threshold, and you will not need to pay for private mortgage insurance on this new loan.

However, like all things, there are pros and cons to refinancing. While it may lower your monthly payment, depending on where you're at in the life of your loan, it could end up costing you more in interest in the long term. Remember, you're essentially taking out a new loan. If you're twenty years into your thirty-year mortgage and choose to refinance—you're actually getting a new thirty-year mortgage.

When applying for a mortgage, we want you to consider the three factors that determine your interest rate. First, interest rates are set by the federal government's fiscal policy. The second factor is your credit history, which most people won't be able to improve much in the short term. The third factor is the one over which you have the most control: the kind of mortgage you select.

The first factor, the interest rate, operates out of your control. It's just a condition of the current financial market. All you can do is look to find the best available mortgage interest rate. The second factor, your creditworthiness, is very important. Establishing and maintaining your credit rating is critical to your ability to qualify for the best interest rate. Some people with slowly improving credit may still qualify for a loan, although it will probably have a higher-than-average interest rate. If you're in this predicament, you have two options: you can either accept the rate and work on improving your scores so you can refinance into a more favorable loan later, or you can fix your credit before buying a home. A good lender can put you in touch with a credit counselor who can help you improve your credit score in the timeliest way.

If your credit score does show up low, immediately check the report for mistakes. Errors are surprisingly common, and many can be cleaned up in a matter of months. If this is the case, you may want to improve your credit before you start seriously looking for a home. It's also important to note that there are some unexpected things that can creep into your credit report, like if you made a recent big purchase or took out another loan. So, no matter how excited you may be about all the purchases that will come along with your new home—like new furniture or silverware—don't fork over the cash for large expenses until *after* the ink is dry. Changing jobs, which will alter your debt-to-income ratio, can also impact or alter your score.

The third factor that will impact your interest rate is the type of mortgage you choose. Mortgages typically fall into two categories: fixed rate and adjustable rate. (More on that later.) Each one has different interest rates that may change over time.

Term

A mortgage loan's term will determine how much interest you pay over the life of the loan and how quickly you build equity by paying it down. As we've discussed before, different mortgages come with different schedules around repayment. In the case of fixed-rate mortgages, loans are scheduled for repayment over larger swaths of time, like fifteen, twenty, or thirty years.

Shorter term loans are good for people who want to build equity quickly and who can afford a higher monthly payment. They dramatically reduce the amount of interest you pay over the life of the loan for two reasons. First, the interest has a shorter amount of time to compound (fifteen years rather than thirty). And second, shorter-term loans usually offer a lower interest rate. The monthly payment on a fifteen-year loan will be higher than on a thirty-year loan, but not by as much as you might expect.

Do the Math: Find the Right Mortgage Term

	15-Year	30-Year	30-Year with Additional $200 Monthly Principal Prepayment
Amount Borrowed	$230,000	$230,000	$230,000
Interest Rate	4%	4%	4%
Monthly Payment	$1,701.28	$1,098.06	$1,298.06
Interest Paid Over Life of Loan	$76,230.80	$165,299.86	$118,379.07
How It Stacks Up	A 15-year mortgage requires a higher monthly payment but dramatically reduces the amount you pay over the life of the loan. Plus, these mortgages usually come with a lower interest rate.	The 30-year term is the most common in the industry. It offers reasonable monthly payments and a reasonable payoff time.	Voluntary prepayment on a 30-year mortgage essentially converts it to a 20-year while allowing you the flexibility to drop to the lower payment level if necessary.

Figure 3.2

However, many buyers who like the idea of quickly building equity may still feel nervous about committing to the higher monthly payment of a shorter-term mortgage. We want you to know you can achieve similar results by taking out a thirty-year mortgage and paying a little extra toward the principal each month. Voluntary prepayment allows you to chip away at your principal faster. It also gives you more flexibility in case of a financial emergency by allowing you to elect not to pay the extra amount that month. And it can have a big impact over time.

Fixed vs. Adjustable Rate

When it comes to mortgages in the United States, there are a couple of different options, but they mostly fall into two categories: **fixed rate** and **adjustable rate**. There are some types of hybrid loans, but, for the most part, loans fall into those two categories.

Fixed rate mortgages are, as the name suggests, mortgages where the interest rate you pay is secured or fixed: the rate you are given at the time you take out the loan is the interest rate you'll have throughout your mortgage's life. (Unless you choose to refinance.) So, if interest rates go up, but you've secured your rate at 4 percent—you still only have to pay that 4 percent interest rate. Though the term of a loan can vary, the two most common term lengths in the United States are a thirty-year and fifteen-year mortgage. (In Canada, the most common fixed rate mortgage loan lasts five years, followed by twenty-five years of variable rates. To get a thirty-year fixed-rate mortgage, you'll have to put down 20 percent.) In other words, you have the option to decide if you prefer paying off your mortgage over a period of fifteen or thirty years. If you choose a fifteen-year mortgage, you'll pay more per month but for a shorter period of time. A thirty-year mortgage will give you a lower monthly payment over a longer period, which also means paying more interest over the life of your loan.

Adjustable-rate mortgages (often referred to as "ARMs"), as the name suggests, have interest rates that fluctuate—or adjust—over the life of the loan. Unlike their fixed-rate counterparts, whatever interest rate you secure at the time the loan starts is only temporary. Usually, the starting rate for an ARM is incredibly low. Then, slowly, depending on the rate index, your interest rate may increase, if rates are on the rise. Fortunately, there are some ways to keep these mortgages from costing an ARM and a leg. Some loans have loan caps that will limit how much the interest rate can increase during the life of the loan, and periodic caps that prevent the rate from increasing too rapidly. In fact, ARMs (called VRMs, or variable-rate mortgages) are one of the most common forms of mortgages in Canada, with the first few years being fixed and then the rate being re-evaluated.

There are some hybrid loans that exist outside of fixed- and adjustable-rate mortgages. Typically, they combine the early benefits of a fixed-rate loan with the limited terms of an ARM. These kinds of loans can be useful for buyers who know they aren't planning on staying in a home forever but still want to get the low rates of an ARM, along with the security of a loan with a fixed rate. That way, these buyers have the benefit of paying something steadily over a pre-agreed upon period of time before the interest rates begin to increase.

The Seven Steps to Financing a Home

Now that we understand what a mortgage *is*, it's time to dive into how to go about finding one and financing your new home. We've broken down the whole financing process into seven basic steps.

The Seven Steps to Financing a Home

1. Establish your budget.
2. Choose the right lender.
3. Apply for a loan and get approved.
4. Decide among your mortgage options.

5. Submit an accepted purchase contract to the lender.

6. Get an appraisal and title.

7. Obtain funding at closing.

Let's walk through each of the seven steps, so you'll be ready to hit the ground running when it's time to make an offer.

1. Establish Your Budget (the Suitcase Principle)

Imagine you're packing to go on vacation. You get out your suitcase and start filling it with T-shirts, shorts, a swimsuit, your toothbrush, and a nice outfit in case you go out for a formal dinner. You pack everything you know you'll need to make your vacation as fun as possible. However, you probably won't pack the suitcase so tight you have to sit on it to get it closed. You know that once you get to your destination—whether it's Boise or Bali—you'll probably find something you want to bring home. So, you leave room for the unknown.

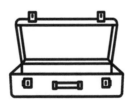

The Suitcase Principle applies to mortgages as well. When you get your preapproval letter, make sure the monthly payment is an amount you feel comfortable paying each month. Lenders are careful, but they make qualification decisions based on averages and formulas.

They won't understand the nuances of your lifestyle and spending patterns quite as well as you do. So, leave a little room in your suitcase for the unexpected. Your new home will give you plenty of opportunities to spend money, from furnishing the guest bedroom to landscaping, if your new home comes with a lawn. "You don't want to be so strapped that you can't go out and buy a flat of flowers," says Mary Anne Collins, an agent in California. "You want to be able to afford the things that make a house a home. If you max out what a loan originator says you can afford, you might not be able to do that."

As a general rule, we recommend spending no more than a third of your gross monthly income on your first home payment. Historically, banks used a ratio called 28/36 to decide how much buyers could borrow. An approved housing payment couldn't be more than 28 percent of the buyer's gross monthly income, or greater than 36 percent of income after their total debt load, including car payments, student loans, and credit card payments. No matter how expensive your market, though, we urge you to think carefully before stretching your personal budget quite so much.

Deciding how much you can afford should also involve some thought about how your financial profile will change in the coming years. If you expect to incur a bunch of new costs—for example, if you plan to start a family—it might be smart to scale back. On the other hand, if you're about to make your final car payment, or send a child from private day care into public kindergarten, you may be able to afford a little more. In the long run, your peace of mind and financial security is what matters most.

The Importance of Preapproval

We recommend getting preapproved as soon as possible—before you start looking at homes. It will give both you and the seller certainty that you can afford the property you want to buy, which can make all the difference in a situation where the seller receives multiple offers. In surveys, many first-time buyers admit the most important thing they should have done was get preapproved sooner. Your real estate agent will ensure you don't put off this important step.

Many loan officers believe that preapproval has become even more critical due to occasional rapid shifts in the mortgage industry. To save time and energy, many suggest you speak with a loan officer before looking at homes; that way you know exactly what you can afford before getting attached to a potential property.

Your Monthly Payment

An important aspect of understanding what you can and can't afford is understanding the nuances of your monthly payment. When you look at how much a house costs and break that down over the life of loan, it may seem like an easy monthly payment. But the reality is there are a number of factors that contribute to what your monthly payment will actually be, both up front and over the life of your loan.

The bulk of your monthly payment will go toward paying off the principal and interest on your mortgage, which is amortized. **Amortization** is the process by which your lender calculates all the interest you will pay over the life of the loan, plus the amount you are borrowing, and divides that by the total number of payments you'll make (for example, a thirty-year loan is 360 monthly payments). Please note, even though every monthly principal and interest payment is exactly the same (if you have the most popular thirty-year, fixed-rate loan), the proportion of principal and interest in each payment varies over time. In the beginning, the bulk of each payment will go toward interest; in later years, more of each payment will go toward paying off the principal (the amount you actually borrowed), thus accelerating your equity buildup.

Understanding Amortization

Principal loan amount:	$240,000
Interest rate:	4.1%
Interest accrued over 30 years:	$177,483.39
Total principal plus interest:	$417,483.39
Divided by 360 monthly payments:	$1,159.68
Annual payment:	$13,916

On top of your principal and interest, each month you will probably pay a portion of your homeowner's **annual insurance premium** and property taxes, which most likely will change from year to year and thereby alter your monthly payment amount.

Property Taxes

Property taxes are important to consider when purchasing a home. Property taxes vary from state to state and city to city. Every year, local governments assess the value of your property, including your home and the land that it sits on. While for some people, property taxes might be minimal, for others they can be incredibly high. In fact, in many cities across the country, property taxes are on the rise. In 2018, for instance, property taxes in the United States rose an average of 4 percent. Generally, people pay around 0.5–2.5 percent of the house purchase price per year. And if the property values in your area are increasing, it's safe to assume your property taxes will go up as well. So, it's important to keep that increase in mind when you pick a place to live. That being said, property taxes are generally deductible up to a certain amount. So, make sure to keep yourself apprised of the most recent tax breaks regarding property taxes.

And property taxes really can make an impact. For instance, in 2018, New Jersey had the highest property taxes at 2.47 percent and Hawaii had the lowest at 0.27 percent. If you purchased a home in Hawaii for $205,000, you would pay roughly $560 annually for property taxes. But in New Jersey, the annual property taxes on that home would be $5,064—that's a big difference!

Because your taxes change each year, in the United States, the monthly payment is often referred to as PITI or PITMI, which stands for Principal, Interest, Taxes, and (Mortgage) Insurance (in Canada it could be referred to as PIT because insurance premiums are rarely included):

- Payments toward the **P**rincipal, which reduces your loan amount
- **I**nterest, which is paid to the lender for allowing you to borrow the money
- Property **T**axes, which are paid to local governments
- Homeowner's **I**nsurance, which is paid to the company that is insuring your home against defined damages and liabilities

Typically, buyers pay PITI to their lender in a single monthly payment. The insurance and tax portions of these funds are then held in **escrow**—a separate, third-party account—until the premiums or taxes are due. In other words, this escrow account works like withholding taxes from your paycheck. It allows you to save throughout the year, so you'll be sure to have enough money to pay annual tax and insurance bills. It also assures the lender that these monies will be paid on time, that there will be no tax default, and that the lender's investment (your home) will be properly insured. Eighty percent of mortgages include escrow payments, and we strongly encourage you to make sure your payments are part of your overall mortgage payment instead of made separately.

Creative Financing

It can seem confusing, expensive, or just plain hard to get a traditional mortgage loan. So, as an option, we'd like to introduce creative financing, a set of time-tested financing strategies that may be available to you regardless of unfavorable economic circumstances, whether general or personal.

Creative financing incorporates a set of strategies that can help you buy a property with less of your own money used as a down payment and may even lower your monthly payment. The following examples represent common ways to execute creative financing.

House-Hacking

As we discussed in Chapter 1, house-hacking can be a creative way to finance a home. With the rise in housing costs, sometimes one of the best ways to afford a home is to split the cost—that's where house-hacking comes in. As a quick refresher, house-hacking involves purchasing a home with the specific goal of renting out a portion of it. This could be as simple as purchasing a two-bedroom home with the intent to rent out the extra room, or as big as purchasing a duplex and renting out the other living space. Having a renter immediately lowers your monthly costs and helps you pay off your mortgage quickly. Moreover, it can reduce expenses, potentially lower your taxable income base, increase your savings, and provide passive income. It offers many of the usual financial benefits of homeownership—such as equity and tax deductions—but with the bonus of having someone to help mitigate the costs.

Washington, D.C., agent James Williams not only encourages his clients to try house-hacking, but used it to buy his own first home. "My story of buying my first home is similar to many of my clients, and I use my experience to share with them ways to increase their income. I purchased my first home in the Philadelphia suburbs. It was a three-level, single-family home with three bedrooms, two and a half bathrooms, and a finished basement. I had a classmate from Duke and a coworker who needed a place to live, so I decided to rent two rooms out. The money I received covered 75 percent of my mortgage and allowed me to pay down on my student loans, save money, and have disposable income. This was the springboard that inspired me to buy investment properties. I have shared this story with many of my clients and they have also bought suitable homes that allowed them to generate income through room rentals."

Cosigners

If house-hacking isn't your style, you can also turn to friends, family, or benefactors who would be willing to help you buy your first home. It's become common for parents or other interested parties to help people purchase their first home. From simply giving an initial lump sum for a down payment, to investing cash to help finance a mortgage, to co-borrowing on the loan, someone can help you financially. If you find yourself wanting to buy a home but are short on the funds, turning to others can help make your dreams of home-ownership come true. However, it's best to either do it with someone you know—like a parent—and document it with a contract.

Piggyback

You can also get creative with financing to get around possible PMI. A common way to get around paying mortgage loan insurance from the start is to take out a second loan, often called a "**piggyback**" in the United States. This is a loan that covers the difference between the cash you have and the cash you need to hit the magical 20 percent mark. For example, if you only have 10 percent to put down, you could take out what's known as an "80/10/10": an 80 percent first loan, a 10 percent second loan, and a 10 percent down payment. Typically, you'll pay a higher rate (particularly on the second loan), but the loan period is usually a shorter period of time. Importantly, because the second loan is a home loan instead of an insurance fee, the interest is tax deductible in the United States, so that means more money in your piggybank.

Other Options

There's also the possibility of you and the seller coming to a unique financing agreement. For instance, a seller may offer what's known as **owner financing**. In this case, the seller owns the home free and clear and offers you a private mortgage loan. Another situation involves your **assumption** of the seller's mortgage. In this scenario, the seller's mortgage lender allows you, the buyer, to take responsibility for the seller's mortgage. (This is most common with things like VA loans.) The last concept is a lease option in which you lease the property from the seller until you have the equity or cash to buy it—sometimes known as "**rent to own**." However, rent to own can be tricky and sometimes not in the renter's best interest. Before agreeing to any rent-to-own program, make sure to be well informed on your legal rights and to consult with a real estate professional.

While owner financing is widely available, please note that not all mortgages are assumable and many mortgages have a due-on-sale clause, meaning that the lender must be notified and give approval for the mortgage to be assumed (sometimes called a "wrap"). Some areas don't permit lease options or their variations: deed for contract and lease purchase. We recommend you ask your agent to connect you with a reputable real estate attorney if you choose any of these creative financing options.

And if you decide to try and take out a private second loan as part of your creative financing strategy, particularly from the seller, it's important you understand the potential pitfalls. You could end up running into what's known as a "**lien**."

What's a Lien?

A lien is a claim against an asset that is used as collateral in the case of a loan or debt. For instance, if you take a loan from a bank to pay for a home but don't ever make your mortgage payment, your lender could put a lien on your home. This means they can claim your home as collateral if you refuse to pay. That way, they can collect a profit on their investment without incurring a financial loss. If things escalate, they can repossess and sell your property. Even small liens will need to be cleared before you can sell your home.

With a second loan comes secondary liens, which usually carry less favorable terms for the buyer—it's about **collateral**. First liens are generally secured against the property and are first in line if the deal goes sour and the property must be liquidated to pay back the loan. Secondary lenders account for this in the terms they offer, which usually involve higher interest rates and shorter terms. The main thing to recognize is that you have many financing options when buying a home. Sometimes you just need to look in less obvious places to find them.

While finding the right mortgage takes a little work, the effort is well worth it. Chosen wisely, your mortgage can be one of your best financial assets. It's what enables you to fulfill the dream of homeownership. It helps ensure your financial security through building equity and net worth. As your equity grows, it will be a valuable source of creditworthiness and financial stability.

2. Choose the Right Lender

Once you know your mortgage loan priorities, you'll be ready to talk to **lenders** about the specific packages they offer. Different lenders can give you a ballpark estimate of the kinds of loans and interest rates you qualify for and the fees they charge.

To begin with, there are a couple different avenues you can take to finding the right lender. Your list of potential loan officers and lenders will likely include both mortgage brokers and mortgage bankers. Either can do a fine job of securing a mortgage for you, but it's helpful to understand the differences between them.

The first option is to work with what is called a "**mortgage broker**." A mortgage broker is someone whose job it is to know and find the best lenders in the market. Mortgage brokers don't actually make (underwrite) loans. Instead, they specialize in shopping the whole mortgage market to find the right loan for their clients. Because they deal with many loan originators, brokers can offer a wider variety of mortgage products. However, because they aren't actually underwriting the loan, it may take longer to get approvals, and they may not be as flexible about the qualifications you'll need.

Or you can go directly to a lender: you can go straight to a bank or other institution to figure out what their loan options are. Once you pick one, you'll work with your lender to get the best deal they have to offer. Mortgage bankers approve and then make their own loans, meaning they're intimately familiar with their company's mortgage products. This enables them to predict with great certainty what their underwriters will approve.

Although it may be tempting to choose a lender

strictly on who quotes you the lowest rate, we recommend prioritizing by a different standard—their reputation. Referrals from friends, your real estate agent, and other people you trust are the best way to find a reputable lender who can get the job done. In the end, having the right lender working for you can assure that all the details are handled in an accurate and timely manner. And you'll trust they are giving you sound financial advice, not just a lot of noise. Your peace of mind is paramount.

Be Ready for Closing Costs

Lender's fees and other closing costs in the United States can add 3–5% to your home's purchase price.

Likely Lender Fees
1. Origination fee ("points")
2. Administration fee
3. Application fee
4. Broker or lender fee
5. Commitment fee
6. Document preparation
7. Underwriting fee

Likely Third-Party Fees
1. Credit report
2. Home appraisal
3. Pest inspections
4. Recording fees
5. Settlement fees
6. Survey
7. Tax and insurance prepayment
8. Title search
9. Title insurance
10. Courier services

And Always Ask
"What other costs will I be responsible for to get our home closed?"

Figure 3.3

After all, the process of finalizing a loan has many steps. Piles of paperwork have to be drawn up, verified, processed, and signed by multiple parties—all within a very short timeframe. Mistakes can delay this process or even derail a loan completely. Nearly every real estate agent has at least one horror story, if not many, about buyers who chose a loan officer and lender based on a low-rate quote, only to find that once they reached closing, certain fees had changed or some rates came out higher. That's why it's important to have a good officer who, while they can't control every rate, has a great head for numbers, knows the market, and can give an accurate estimate.

What Differences Do Fees Make?

While fees are rarely associated with home loans in Canada, in the United States they are commonplace. It's important that you understand what those fees are, so you aren't taken by surprise at closing. "Many clients do not realize there are closing costs on top of a down payment," explains loan officer Monica Jenkins. "So, having a clear expectation of what is needed to close is important."

On closing day in the United States, you will probably be responsible for various fees and expenses on top of your down payment. These closing costs are explained in more detail in Chapter 8. Closing costs include the lender's own fees and third-party fees for requirements such as title insurance and the cost of prepaying a year's worth of property insurance. Because closing costs can be in the thousands of dollars, it's a good idea to compare what different lenders charge. Line-by-line comparisons can be confusing, so instead, when you get your loan estimates, we suggest you compare the total costs. If Lender A is more expensive than Lender B, don't be afraid to ask why. Sometimes lenders will negotiate.

Another important thing to remember are "points." A point is a fee attached to the loan that equals 1 percent of the principal of the loan. One point on a $100,000 loan equals $1,000. Many loans include the cost of points up front in exchange for a slightly lower interest rate, which usually shows up as an origination fee. In high-interest-rate environments, buyers sometimes pay extra points to buy a lower interest rate. However, this strategy only pays off over a longer period. For example, you wouldn't want to pay thousands up front to save $100 or so a month if you were going to move in a few years—there's just no point. So, if you're considering paying points, we suggest you ask your lender or agent to walk you through the math, point by point, just to make sure it's worth the investment.

We know great loan officers and their lenders can work wonders. They can even save you from a bad loan. That's why it's important to do your due diligence when it comes to selecting one. Agent Jennifer Barnes of Atlanta, Georgia, worked with a couple whose lender was missing in action on closing day. "When we got to the closing table, there was no one to be found," she says. "There was no loan package, no nothing." Jennifer snapped into action to get a new loan processed in less than a week, relying on her strong relationship with a lending team. "I knew an appraiser who would drop everything and handle it. Then it was just a matter of getting it approved," she adds.

In short, just like your agent, your lender matters. So, keep yourself safe: start your loan search by shopping referrals, not rates. Of course, rates and fees do matter. But the right loan officer will let you know ahead of time all of the rates and fees for their lender's loan products you are considering, so you'll know if they are fair and competitive. In the end, the lender will provide you a loan estimate that details the loan officer's best forecast of what you qualify for, what interest rate you can get, and all the fees involved.

3. Apply for a Loan and Get Approved

Now that you've found your mortgage partner, the next step is to fill out an application and get preapproved. The best way to know what exactly you can afford to buy is to get approved for a loan. Getting approved for a loan before you've even picked a house is called "**preapproval**," and it's one of the best ways to get a house, particularly in a hot market. Getting approved for a loan is a relatively straightforward process that mostly requires finding a lender you like and getting together the right documents.

Preapproval will let you know the most you can borrow—and when added to your down payment, it sets a ceiling for your price range. But, as you know, there's more to a home than just a ceiling. However, to really pinpoint your target home purchase price, don't simply rely on your lender's preapproval. Talk it over with your real estate agent or your financial adviser. Lenders determine what you can borrow, but only you can decide what you can afford. First-time home buyer Jeffrey Barg of Philadelphia, Pennsylvania, decided to consult with a financial planner on how much he should invest in his home purchase. "Since I wasn't leaving Philadelphia anytime soon, buying a home made financial sense. My planner confirmed this and helped me figure out how much I could spend. I used that information as a guideline," says Jeffrey.

Preapproval Documents Checklist

When it comes time to apply for a loan, you want to make sure you have every document you might need at hand. That way, the process will go as smoothly as possible. To apply, you'll need:

1. **Proof of income and employment:** If you work for a company, most likely that will mean providing a W-2. For self-employed workers, this could mean providing your latest 1099.

2. **Information on debts:** Have you taken out a loan to pay for a car or have student loan debt? (Who doesn't these days?) You'll need documentation so that loan processes can calculate your debt-to-income ratio.

3. **Information on additional assets:** You'll also want to make sure you have documentation for any other assets you might have. That can include retirement accounts, pensions, or any other finances you have access to.

If you live in Canada, your checklist will be a little different. For instance, proof of employment can come in the form of an employment letter, a T4, a general tax return, or a notice of assessment.

To make sure you don't get in over your head, lending institutions carefully analyze your finances to come up with a reasonable guess of what you can afford. To start this process, you submit an application to a lender detailing your income, assets, and debts. The officer will help you explore your financing options and figure out roughly how much you can borrow and the kind of loan that will work best for you.

Once you have a general game plan, your application goes to an underwriter who makes sure all the information checks out and then decides exactly how much the institution is willing to lend you. The is the preapproval process. The application will take about an hour of your time. Underwriting usually takes a few days. Computerized underwriting has actually allowed for some applications to be completed and approved in a matter of hours, but it is generally wise to expect it to take longer. We consider preapproval paramount to your home-buying success, and we discuss it at several points throughout this chapter.

Understanding Credit

You've found a house and a lender—now it's time to apply for that mortgage. But what about your credit? What is your credit score, and how will it impact your mortgage?

Credit scores are a measure of our creditworthiness. A fair bit can go into your credit scores, from paying your rent on time to getting a new credit card. The main ingredients that make up your score are payment history, your amount of debt, amount of new credit, the length of your credit history, and your credit mix. For instance, if you pay all of your credit card bills on time—you'll have a good score on your payment history. But if you keep getting new credit cards, ask for a higher credit limit, or even get your credit score pulled for a credit report, these actions could impact your credit score in the short term. What you want is a steady, long history of good credit with little debt.

The top three entities that create and monitor credit scores are FICO, Experian, and TransUnion. Each company has a series of different ways to measure your credit that apply for different purchases. When it comes time to getting your mortgage, most lenders will pull your FICO scores to determine your loan options. The better your credit score, the more loans will be available to you and the better interest rates you'll have access to.

That isn't to say if your credit score is low, you can't buy a house—you certainly can! But the loans available to you will be fewer, and you may have to get more creative with your financing. Earlier in this chapter, we looked at some creative financing options that may be available to you if a poor credit score has made conventional financing unattractive or un-available. And remember, if you want a copy of your credit report that won't harm your score, you can pull a free copy once a year through *annualcreditreport.com*.

4. Decide among Your Mortgage Options

A down payment, an interest rate, and the time over which you pay back your loan—that's the basic recipe for a mortgage loan. Even though all mortgages have the same ingredients, you can blend them in a myriad of ways to serve your financial needs. We hope you remember that the kind of mortgage you choose will shape how much you pay up front, how much you pay each month, and how much interest you pay over the life of the loan. You decide which of these factors are most important to you:

I want a low monthly payment.
There are two fundamental ways to achieve a low monthly payment: you buy less home or pay more up front. Most people choose the latter. A larger down payment will reduce your total loan amount and may help you secure a better rate. Depending on where interest rates are, what your long-term plans are, and

how you feel about risk, you might also consider an adjustable-rate mortgage or one with a longer term.

I want to put as little down as possible.
As a first-time home buyer, it's important to remember there are a variety of options and plans that can help you get your home while putting down less than 20 percent. Just make sure to talk to your agent and broker and do your due diligence.

I want to build up equity quickly.
Consider a loan amortized over fifteen years or take out a thirty-year mortgage and make voluntary prepayments. These are also good choices if you value paying less interest over the life of the loan and building up the equity you have in the home. This can positively impact your financial net worth and your creditworthiness.

I want to minimize risk.
A thirty-year fixed-rate loan with a 20 percent down payment is probably your safest option. You move in with equity already in the property, and your interest rate is locked in for the life of the loan, no matter how high interest rates may climb after you move in.

As a first-time home buyer, consider all your options carefully, including government-sponsored first-time buyer programs. We think you'll enjoy the benefits these programs offer and thank yourself for years to come.

5. Submit an Accepted Purchase Contract to the Lender

You've found your home, been preapproved by a lender, made an offer, and had it accepted—huzzah! In most cases, that means putting together an accepted purchase contract. This contract clearly lays out everything for the sale of the house, from what will stay in the home to the timeline for the sale.

In essence, this contract will outline all terms, conditions, and contingencies for the sale of the home. Once this has been signed and agreed upon, you'll need to submit it to your lender to move the process along. Chapter 6 gives more detail on everything that goes into making a strong offer and hammering out the details of the transaction. But wait—don't jump ahead yet! There's a bunch of other stuff we want to tell you first.

6. Get an Appraisal and Title

When it comes time to close, there are two things that need to happen: get the property appraised and make sure the title is clear. But what does that even mean?

An appraisal is a way for the lender to understand the value of your property before finalizing your loan. This protects the lender from loaning too much (or too little) for the property. For example, most banks don't want to shell out half a million dollars for a property that is only appraised for around $250,000—that would be irresponsible.

Title is simply the legal rights to a property. If you're going to buy the house, you need to make sure that the people selling it to you, well, can. That's why most lenders have a dedicated team to help research and transfer the title. The title search is where you'll verify that no one else has placed a lien on the property. Luckily, if you find out that the title does not, in fact, belong to the seller, there are clauses to make sure you can get out of the deal. (This will be covered more in-depth in Chapters 6 and 8.)

7. Obtain Funding at Closing

The final countdown has begun! You've made your offer, signed the contracts, and gotten everything inspected. Your *i's* are dotted and your *t's* are crossed, which means all that is left is obtaining funding at closing. This is the part where the lender does final verification and approval for the loan. Once everything gets the go-ahead and papers are signed, the loan becomes officially yours.

This whole process—from preapproval to funding—generally takes place over several months, though the timeline varies from deal to deal. As always, one of the best ways to stay on top of everything is to make sure you get preapproved and have all of your documentation in order. But before we get to closing (and all of the paperwork), we need to, ya know, find a home.

Notes to Take Home

- Follow these seven steps to financing your home:

  1. Establish your budget.

  2. Choose the right lender.

  3. Apply for a loan and get approved.

  4. Decide among your mortgage options.

  5. Submit an accepted purchase contract to the lender.

  6. Get an appraisal and title.

  7. Obtain funding at closing.

- You don't need to save up a lot of money for the down payment. A conventional mortgage can require as little as 5 percent, and there are even some first-time buyer programs that require even less.

- Having the right loan officer (or mortgage specialist) working for you assures that all the details will be handled in an accurate and timely manner and that you will receive sound financial advice.

- Lenders determine what you can borrow, but only you can decide what you can afford.

- Understanding the three basic parts of a mortgage loan—down payment, interest rate, and terms—will help you choose the best one for you.

- Visit *YourFirstHomeBook.com* for worksheets and other helpful resources.

GARY KELLER'S FIRST HOME

We moved around a lot when I was a boy growing up in Houston, Texas, but some of my fondest memories are of my very first childhood home—which was also my parents' first home to own. It was one of those sturdy tract houses you saw everywhere in the 1950s—three tiny bedrooms, two baths with shiny, pastel-colored tiles on the walls, a small den, and a tight two-car garage.

Our home stood on Dorothy Street, surrounded by others that were almost identical, separated by chain-link fences that kept kids and pets safe but still freely invited conversations between neighbors. Each lawn was mowed and manicured. It was a great place to grow up.

When I think of that house, so many heartfelt memories come to mind. My dad playing with us on the hardwood floor and tossing us up in the air. Our huge,

---

Photograph courtesy of the Keller family.

solid swing set in the backyard—not one of those light-weight ones that rocks back and forth. Dad bought ours from a place that sold park playground equipment and then cemented it into the ground. It had swings, a slide, monkey bars, and even a trapeze, and it set the stage for many adventures. He also built a sandbox next to it, and my buddies and I spent hours there building tunnels and playing with our plastic cars and trucks. We built elaborate backyard forts, using cardboard boxes we scavenged from the nearby furniture store. Each summer, Dad put up a blue plastic pool that would hold seven or eight kids. Everyone in the neighborhood congregated there.

I can still see my mother standing at the back fence, talking to our neighbor Mrs. Ramsey, and my father, with a bandana around his head, mowing the lawn in his plaid shorts, dress shoes, and dark socks—dads didn't wear tennis shoes back then. I remember the cozy, wood-paneled breakfast nook with a Formica table where we gathered for meals, and where my mother once washed my mouth out with soap for saying something she thought was disrespectful. ("Bet your booties" was obviously cussing, according to my Mom!) I recall birthdays and holidays, especially the aluminum Christmas tree with the color wheel—my two sisters and I spent hours watching the tree change colors as the wheel turned. Dad built a workshop in the backyard. He had someone pour the concrete foundation, and he constructed the rest. I carried his tools, and it was there I first learned to hammer nails. Building the workshop took him a year, and although it was only 12 foot by 12 foot, I thought it was huge. I was in awe of what my dad created.

A home is a place that houses your most powerful memories. You can reminisce about a rental, but you'll never think of it in the same way. Living in your first home just may be the most exhilarating material experience you can ever have. Nothing else quite compares. It's where you hang your hat, where you rest your head; it's a source of warmth and security and can become a solid investment in your financial future. Your home is where you build a workshop or cement a swing set into the ground or plant a rose garden like my dad and I did. There really is no place like home, especially when it's your own—especially if it's on Dorothy Street.

Gary Keller is the executive chairman and cofounder of Keller Williams Realty.

CHAPTER 4

IDENTIFY YOUR CRITERIA

When Cheri Corrado was looking for her first home, she thought she knew exactly what she wanted. She was a real estate agent, after all, and knew her Washington, D.C., market inside out. She wanted a detached single-family home, not one of the townhomes common in her area. She searched for weeks, fruitlessly, before a chance conversation with another agent at her office changed everything.

"I was telling her about the trouble I was having," says Cheri, "and she asked, 'Well, why do you want a single-family house?'"

Cheri thought about it and was stunned to realize that she didn't want a single-family home. She didn't particularly like yard work and didn't have time for it anyway. What she wanted, she discovered, was as much square footage as possible. She had assumed that detached single-family homes would get her the most space.

"Once I realized that what I most wanted in a home was size, I could stop looking for a detached home and start looking for space," she says. She soon found a townhome she absolutely loved. "That's why you need to get down to *why* you want what you want."

You may think that shopping for homes starts with jumping in the car and driving all over town or scrolling through new listings on the Internet. And it's true that this can be the most exciting part of the home-buying process. All those properties! All those neighborhoods! All those weird pictures of listings where you wonder how the owner thought their design choices and renovations would possibly make people want to buy their house?! In fact, most people have been looking for homes online well before they've considered actually purchasing one on their own. Because a new home is an amazing prospect—it means new dreams and new possibilities.

But when it comes time to buy your first home, it's important to put some of those lofty expectations aside. According to Houston, Texas, agent Lance Loken, "A buyer's first house is rarely their forever home and may not hit all of their desired criteria. But it is usually a stepping-stone in their real estate journey." Most of us can't afford that dream library or heated pool just yet. That's why looking for homes actually begins with carefully assessing your values, wants, and needs for the short and long term. For Rancho Mirage, California, agent Brady Sandahl, this kind of consultation is invaluable. He says "I ask home buyers a series of questions about what is driving them to purchase something new and why those driving factors are so important. For example, if they say they want a four-bedroom home, I will ask 'Great! Who or how will you enjoy each of the four bedrooms?' Remember, look for the reason (or what I call the ingredient) causing you to lean in that direction."

In the home-buying process, an initial consultation with your agent is your way to make sure you are prepared. You may think you already have a pretty good idea of what your first home might look like, and you're probably right. However, you want to be sure you haven't missed something. That's why it's important to sit down, talk through things with your agent, and even sign a **buyer representation agreement**. As Cheri Corrado learned, you can't be absolutely sure what you really need until you take the time to get down to the *why*.

Going from "What" to "Why"

When we say you need to get down to the why, that's another way of saying you need to figure out what you value most and how your first home can embody those values. We need to break down the notion of what we want into smaller pieces to help us understand the underlying why.

During your consultation, we challenge you to set aside any preconceptions you may have about what you want and the homes that are available. Then, beginning with a clean slate, you should assemble a list of search criteria that reflects what you truly need.

First, let's clear up what we mean when we say, "underlying why." Your why is informed by your values so that you can identify what it is you need and what it is that you want. By "values," we mean those broad, overall considerations that are the bedrock of your personal desires—privacy, safety, good schools, time outdoors, entertaining at home, and enough space. Your values shape your specific needs—a large yard, room to entertain, or a short commute. These will inform your more specific wants. Wants are the particular ways you'd like to meet your needs. For example, to fulfill your need for a short commute, you may have a specific neighborhood in mind. Or your wants may be things you like, such as granite countertops or access to a local green space.

Now, use the form in the Appendix page 251 and write down everything you want in a home. (Or, if you'd prefer, write it on a piece of paper or make a list on a computer. This is about what you want, after all.) Jot down everything you can think of: size, neighborhood, architectural style, amenities, everything. Once you have your list of whats, you can start getting down to the why.

Here's how this process might work. Let's say that right at the top of your list is your desire to live in the Southwest Woods neighborhood. Nowhere else will do. Unfortunately, Southwest Woods is so expensive that the only thing you could afford to buy there would be a home barely big enough for you and your falcon Mordecai, let alone your partner and future kids. As you sit at your kitchen table between your partner and agent, with Mordecai perched on your shoulder, your agent asks why you want to live in that particular neighborhood.

"I just really like Southwest Woods," you say. "It's where I've always dreamed of living." But what is it that you like about Southwest Woods specifically? If it's the schools, for instance, you may need to consider other factors. In this instance, your why is education, and you see a Southwest Woods address as a way to achieve a good one. But do you even have children yet? And if so, how old are they?

If you don't have children or they're very young, you don't need to be concerned with great schools just yet. It could be five years or more before you even have a child in school. In a situation like this, you might consider whether this is the home you expect to live in when that want turns into a need. If it is, then Southwest Woods clearly may be your best option. If not, maybe you should put your more immediate needs at the top of the list, like a home that has high ceilings for Mordecai to enjoy.

As you explore your needs, be sure to separate them into immediate short-term needs and anticipated future needs, such as room to start a family or a new home business. In North America, roughly 14 percent of the population tends to move every year. Put another way, according to US Census data, the average person can expect to move 11.7 times in their lifetime. That means moving roughly every seven years. So, it's very likely that some of your long-term wants can move off your list of short-term needs. You and your agent should begin your consultation by discussing your values.

Get Clear about Your Criteria: Questions to Ask
This is the point at which many home-buying books would offer an exhaustive list of possible features and characteristics to consider when shopping for a home. We're not going to do that. We believe it's best for you to focus on the options available within your local market, rather than trying to make sense of rules that are supposed to apply anywhere. Hard and fast rules are usually difficult and slow, and they never apply everywhere anyway. Instead, we offer questions that

help you evaluate and prioritize the things you want and need from your first home. Our goal is to help you define the criteria that will find you a home that meets all your needs and as many of your wants as possible.

1. What Do I Want My Home To Be Close to? What Do I Want My Neighborhood To Be Like?

There are two ways to think about location: proximity and character. "Proximity" means the areas that are geographically desirable to you: they're close to your job, your friends and family, local schools, and city amenities, among other things. However, the question of location also encompasses character: the kind of homes, streets, and parks that a given area has to offer. For example, you may want a downtown condo because you like the bustle of urban life, not because the area is close to anything in particular. Someone else may want an older home and be willing to look in any part of town as long as it's historic.

So, when you discuss location with your agent, we advise you to separate proximity from character so you can better prioritize your needs. Some people may be willing to drive farther to work so they can live in that historic neighborhood on the hill. Others want the fastest commute possible so they can get home to their families.

Fayetteville, Arkansas, agent Mike Duley explores the geographic needs of his buyers in literal terms. "It really depends on the clients' long-term goals. A property that has more acreage can be a benefit for clients who are going to expand their family or are looking for a vacation home or a rental. Plus, with folks working from home more, Internet connectivity is also important to consider." Through conversation, Duley learns about his clients' specific needs and wants, while his clients learn more about the realities of the market. Armed with a clearer perspective, his clients can undertake a more targeted home search and make a more informed buying decision.

2. How Much Space Do I Need?
What Do I Need That Space For?

It's not enough to say that you want a four-bedroom home. A 1,200-square-foot four-bedroom ranch house built in 1950 will offer far less space than a more contemporary four-bedroom home that could easily have double the square footage. A smaller home may be a fine starter home for a family with their first baby on the way. However, it would be a poor choice if you're planning to stay there so long that your growing family will start climbing the walls.

While many people judge the size of a house by the number of bedrooms it has, it's important to think carefully about what you want the space for. Maybe you like to entertain, and an open floor plan is more important than extra bedrooms. Or maybe you want room for a home office—and a converted basement or garage could do the trick just as well as an extra bedroom. So, the question of size encompasses both how much and what kind of space you need.

3. What Is Most Important: Location or Size?

The nicer the neighborhood, the more expensive the homes. Everyone knows that. Most first-time buyers have to settle for a trade-off between size and location. Some people may prefer a smaller home in a nicer area, while others would rather have more square footage, even if the neighborhood's not quite as fashionable.

4. Would I Be Interested in a Fixer-Upper?

One possible way to get as much space as you want in the neighborhood you love is by taking on a fixer-upper. Transforming a run-down property from eyesore to eye-opener can be financially and personally rewarding. However, before you add "fixer-upper" to your list of criteria, we want you to make sure you know what you're getting into. We know that the bevy of fixer-upper-based shows tend to make renovating seem like a smart, inexpensive path to your dream home, but that isn't always the case.

A fixer-upper isn't necessarily a deal if you end up putting more money into the repairs than you saved on the purchase price. Buying a property in poor condition may be a longer, more complicated process as you call in specialists for estimates on what it will cost to update that 1970s kitchen, fix the foundation, or put in new floors. The reality is there's a big difference between making small cosmetic changes, like painting the walls or laying down floors, and bigger structural changes. If you don't have the time, patience, or talent for the project, you may not be happy taking on the home-improvement challenge.

5. What Kind of Property Should I Buy?

Around 83 percent of all homes sold are what agents call a "detached single-family residence." In plain English, that's what most people call "a house." But a house isn't the only choice available—there are townhouses, duplexes, condominiums, and more. In truth, no matter where you are or what you're looking for, there's likely a type of property that will fit perfectly into your lifestyles or finances (and hopefully both). You may want to consider a few of these alternatives to the classic single-family home.

Condominiums

Many people think of condos as downtown high-rises. However, the term "**condominium**" doesn't refer to a particular kind of construction. Instead, the term refers to a form of shared ownership. When you buy a condo, you're buying your own space within a building. And when we say "space," we mean space: condo owners usually don't actually own the walls, floor, or ceiling—they own the space inside. Maintenance costs are shared, and maintenance headaches are handled by a board of directors elected by the condo members. This makes them ideal for people who don't want the hassles of home maintenance, dislike yard work, or simply like the idea of belonging to a community. Many condos also have amenities like swimming pools and playgrounds that many single-family homes lack. And, even though on average, condos cost slightly more per square foot than detached single-family homes, in many cities condos are among the most affordable properties on the market.

Condos aren't for everyone. For one thing, they have rules, usually called "**CC&Rs**" (covenants, conditions, and restrictions). CC&Rs vary from community to community: they may govern how many pets or vehicles you can have, what you can store on your patio, or rules concerning noise levels. So, before you commit to a condo, make sure you can live with the rules. Also, make sure you understand the fees associated with owning a condo, which cover the maintenance, the general property insurance, and upkeep of things such as the plumbing or the roof. Fees are not generally on an as-needed basis. Rather, they're usually fixed and are due every month or quarter. You may not consider this an annoyance, but there is a flip side of not having to deal with maintenance. You have very little control—if the rest of the members decide to let the property slide into disrepair, there's not much you can do but try to sell before it's too late.

Townhomes

Townhouses offer many of the same luxuries of both condos and single-family homes. They're larger and tend to have either a small or no yard and are generally found in urban areas. However, unlike condos where you are often in a more apartment-like setting, townhouses are set up more like houses with adjoining walls. Architecturally speaking, townhomes are just condensed single-family homes. Generally, they're multilevel, with the living room, dining room, and kitchens on the first floor and bedrooms on the second or third.

However, townhouses tend to have fewer offered communal amenities than condos. So, if you're wanting something with access to a pool or a close-knit community, townhomes may not be the right choice for you. But if you want the square footage of a house, little to no yard work, and an urban location—there are few better options. However, many townhomes also have **HOAs**, or homeowner's associations. That means you'll need to pay monthly dues and follow community rules. In many cases, it also means any changes you wish to make to the exterior of your home or yard will have to be approved by the HOA.

Duplexes/Triplexes

Duplexes and triplexes can be incredible investment properties and are particularly useful if you want to try your hand at house-hacking. Essentially, duplexes and triplexes are multiple homes under one roof. So, if you're wanting to buy a property but pay off your mortgage faster or make more income, there are fewer better options on the market. For instance, you could choose to live in one part of the duplex and rent out the other half. This way, you have someone else helping to cover your mortgage, HOA fees, and utilities.

However, the more units the building has, the more its construction lends itself to investors as opposed to homeowners. Triplexes and quadplexes are often less dolled up and more functional, designed to appeal to someone who is looking to use the property purely as an investment and not as their own home. So, make sure to take the time when considering larger multi-unit properties and think of how much work you want to put in to making it livable for yourself and the other tenants. What level of responsibility as a landlord are you willing to take on? How much time do you want to invest in the property? If the answers lean more toward less time, money, or energy—the fewer units the better.

6. Would I Be Interested in New Home Construction?

For some buyers, nothing beats brand-new construction. And, frankly, there's a lot to love! New homes have the latest features and floor plans, so you don't have to worry about old appliances or outdated bathrooms. They're often the best way to maximize square footage because they're built farther out of town where land is more readily available. Frequently, you get to customize your home's décor, and new subdivisions often have amenities like swimming pools, parks, running trails, and security gates, which older neighborhoods may lack.

However, new construction still comes with some special concerns. Like condos, about 80 percent of houses in new developments in the United States require buyers to join and pay fees toward an HOA. That means living by the CC&Rs. Many people appreciate these rules because they protect property values by keeping the neighborhood tidy and pleasant. However, some home-owners find them nitpicky, and annoying disputes over community rules have even led to lawsuits over residents' rights to fly a flag, put in a doghouse, or display political signs, to name just a few examples.

If a brand-new home is a top priority, this will shape your search for a location. We want to remind you that the newest homes are often on the outskirts of town, which may be convenient if you work in a suburban office park but may be excruciating if your job is downtown. Also, opting for new construction can have implications if you plan to move. Like condos that lose their luster when a newer building goes in next door, it can some-times be hard to sell a gently used home when buyers have the alternative of a new one in the next subdivision down the road.

7. What Features Do I Need? What Amenities Do I Want?
Your lifestyle determines the kind of features you really need your home to have. If you have four kids, you *need* a lot of bedrooms; if you have four Alaskan malamutes, you *need* a big yard. You might need a living area big enough for a grand piano, wide doorways to accommo-date a wheelchair, enough bathrooms for litter boxes

for your clowder of cats, and a big garage to tinker with your vintage car. "It is so important to understand who will be enjoying the home and how—and this includes our four-legged family members, too!" notes agent Brady Sandahl. "I love having buyers open up their daily schedules and peel back the curtain so that I understand what their average day looks like. This helps me see what pain points exist or what conveniences or luxuries they are accustomed to."

Analyze What You Want and What You Need in a Home's Features and Amenities

Features

- Age: Do you prefer historic properties or newer ones?
- Style: Do you have a special preference for ranches, bungalows, or another style of construction?
- Bedrooms: How many?
- Bathrooms: How many? Are they updated?
- Living and dining areas: A traditional, formal layout or a more open, contemporary plan?
- Stories: How many?
- Square feet: How much space?
- Ceilings: How high?
- Kitchen: How big? Recently updated? Open to the other living areas?
- Storage: Big closets, a shed, an extra-large garage?
- Parking: A garage or carport? Room for how many vehicles?
- Extras: Attic or basement?

Amenities

- Office
- Play/exercise room
- Security System
- Sprinkler
- Workshop/studio
- In-law suite
- Fireplace
- Pool
- Hot tub
- Sidewalk
- Wooded lot
- Patio, deck, or porch
- Laundry room

Figure 4.1

Homes come with a dizzying variety of features and amenities—that's what makes searching for the right one so much fun! Your dream home may have high ceilings or wood floors, luxurious carpets or big windows, a pool or a fireplace, vintage or flashy countertops. But as you're envisioning all the wonderful things you want your home to have, we want you to be very careful to separate those that you truly need—like those four bed-rooms—from those you could do without. Most homes simply won't have it all. So, you'll have to decide what you value most, and go from there.

8. What Does My Home Have to Have Now? What Does It Have to Have the Potential For?

There are some things you can't change about a prop-erty, such as its age or location, and some that are expensive to change, such as size or layout. Still, there are a myriad of changes and alterations you can make to create your own personalized space. As you're deciding which of your wants are true needs, remember that part of the joy of owning your own home is being able to keep making it better and better.

Some of your needs, then, will be things the home doesn't have to have today—but has to have the *potential* for. Maybe you don't need a home with lush landscaping, for example, but you do need a yard with good sunlight and room to put in a garden. Maybe you don't need a big, screened-in porch right now, but you do need a layout and lot that would work with the porch or deck you someday hope to add. So, we encourage you to make a special list of needs for potential items that may inform your decision.

9. Of All My Wants and Needs, Which Are the Most Important?

As you can clearly see, you'll need to prioritize. Your needs come first, of course, but then you should sort through your wants and decide which are the most important. Agent Lance Loken offers the following guideline for first-time home buyers: "Before purchasing a home, buyers should consider the following: Does this home at least meet my top three criteria and budget?" We suggest you don't take anything off the list—your agent should know to keep an eye out for those quartz countertops or built-in bookshelves that make you swoon. But your focus should be on the must-haves, with the want-to-haves or the nice-to-haves coming last.

Your Home Wants and Needs Criteria

1. Location
2. Size
3. Condition
4. Appreciation
5. Neighborhood
6. Freestanding or condo/townhome, duplex or triplex, resale, or new construction
7. Features and amenities
8. Potential for expansion or improvement

Kailey Humphries and her husband were aspiring first-time home buyers in Calgary, Alberta, with a unique need for space. Working with their agent, Debra Komitsch, they had been looking for a few months. They knew they wanted a townhome-style property. And while they were willing to compromise on certain aspects of their first home, they really needed all the free storage space they could find.

"My husband and I are members of the Canadian National Bobsled team, so we have a lot of equipment and we needed space for it. We knew a garage or a basement was a necessity," Kailey recalls. After their need for storage space, location was their next priority. Since their training facility and work location are in the same area, they didn't want a long commute to either site.

"We were not too picky on the overall size of the place, but we ideally wanted two bedrooms, two bathrooms, and a garage for storage close to where we trained and worked." Debbie found them the perfect solution—a 1,200-square-foot home with two bedrooms, two and a half bathrooms, and a single-car garage. "And within ten minutes of where we train and work!" says Kailey.

You've Got Your House Criteria . . . Now What?

As you can see, there are many factors to consider when setting your criteria. But even after you've figured out what you want to spend, what you're looking for, and where you're willing to compromise, what happens next? What will be the process for your home search and for making an offer?

So, before you leave this initial consultation, ask your agent for the next steps to finding a home that fits your criteria and timetable. That means asking:

- *What kind of home are we searching for?* Ask your agent to reiterate what you're looking for so you can clarify any points of confusion.
- *How will we be notified of new properties?* You may get a daily email through an app or portal, or you may get a phone call a few times a week. Find out how and when you can expect to be informed.

- *What are the rules of our local real estate market?* You need to be prepared for the offer process before you find a home you love. This is particularly important if you're in a hot market where you may need to act quickly. (See Chapter 6 for more information.)

Use the Consultation to Learn Your Market

As your agent helps you probe what you're looking for in a home, make sure you take the opportunity to understand the rules of your unique market. Consider the following questions:

1. How fast are homes selling in my price range?

2. What kinds of homes are selling the fastest?

3. Am I likely to face a multiple-offer situation?

4. What should I expect to include in an offer to help it get accepted?

5. What kind of terms and conditions are typically included in a contract? (A detailed discussion of offer writing comes in Chapter 6.)

Now that you've done the hard work of thinking deeply about your wants and needs and establishing criteria for your search, you're about to start the most thrilling part of the home-buying journey: home tours. As you and your agent begin to explore these houses and imagine your future life there, use the advice in the following chapter to help make finding that home a bit easier.

Notes to Take Home

- A consultation with your agent is the way to pinpoint what you are looking for. The right house will meet all your important needs and as many of your additional wants as possible.

- The questions you should ask yourself include:

  - What do I want my home to be close to? What do I want my neighborhood to be like?

  - How much space do I need? What do I need that space for?

  - Which is more critical: location or size?

  - Would I be interested in a fixer-upper?

  - What kind of property should I buy?

  - Would I be interested in new home construction?

  - What features do I need? What amenities do I want?

  - What does my home have to have now? What does it have to have the potential for?

  - Of all my wants and needs, which are the most important?

GARY GENTRY'S FIRST HOME

When I think of my childhood and family over the years, my mind is immediately filled with images of the places we lived. As a baby, I lived in one of the three houses that my grandfather built on a large lot he owned in the small town of Henrietta, Texas. He was a lumberyard owner and builder, and my parents rented from him. When I was four, we left Henrietta for McKinney, Texas, and my parents purchased their first home. I keenly remember my dad giving me a paint brush to help him paint that house. Since my father was a pilot for the Air Force, we moved around quite a bit when I was growing up. In the fourth grade alone, I attended schools in San Francisco, California; Waco, Texas; West Palm Beach, Florida; and Mountain Home, Idaho; so homeownership wasn't always an option for my parents.

Photograph courtesy of the Gentry family.

My wife, Melondie, and I were college sweethearts. After we graduated from Baylor University, we stayed in Waco and rented an apartment. Although neither of us made much money, we knew we wanted to buy a house. We managed to save every cent from Mel's paychecks for a couple of years in order to have a down payment.

Making a big-ticket purchase like a house can be scary, but it's not risky when you have good counsel. When the time came for us to start our home search, we found a wonderful real estate agent. In fact, I credit her with inspiring my own real estate career. She helped us pinpoint exactly what we were looking for—the smallest house in the nicest neighborhood. Our first home at 3630 Chateau was exactly that.

I can picture our first home in my mind like a portrait. Built in 1946, it was a one-story home with two bedrooms and a nice, large yard. It wasn't big, only about 1,600 square feet, but it was the right size for us, and we had a vision for what it could be. When we purchased it in 1976 for $33,000, we put 30 percent down and had a twenty-year loan at 9 percent interest.

Some of my favorite memories are of remodeling that house. We didn't have much money, so everything that needed to be done we learned how to do ourselves. We sanded, stained, and refinished the hardwood floors. We painted the interior of the house, removed wallpaper, enlarged closets, enclosed a breezeway, and updated the bathrooms and kitchen. Mel and I made it our own.

Our first house was so much more than an address—it was where we really became a family. All of our memories of being a young family are part of that home. Both of our daughters were born while we lived there. I remember mowing the grass while my daughter watched from a playpen under the big trees in the yard. Mel and I still laugh about the time we saw our oldest daughter teach a friend her game, "Let's remodel the house," where they got to work sandpapering scrap pieces of wood.

The biggest lesson we learned with our first home was the realization that a house doesn't just need to satisfy your emotional and physical needs—it also needs to be a great investment. Our agent served us well, teaching us about the importance of location, the bones of the home, and what's around it. We took all of this into consideration when we purchased the home at 3630 Chateau. When we sold it four years later, it had already appreciated from $33,000 to $89,000. We put in the sweat equity to get it into great shape and derive the financial benefits, and this was well before Chip and Joanna Gaines ever arrived on the scene! The positive lessons we learned about investing will stay with us forever, just like our wonderful family memories in our first home.

Gary Gentry was the first Keller Williams real estate agent and has been in the business for decades, helping thousands of clients find their dream homes.

CHAPTER 5

FIND YOUR HOME

Searching for homes is a little like dating: you have a pretty good idea what will make a good match, but you never know exactly when the sparks will fly. You might spend a few weeks combing the market, or you might fall in love your first trip out. No matter how long it takes or how many stops there are on your journey, finding the right home to make an offer on is essentially a four-step process:

1. Determine what houses you want to see.
2. Check out homes that match your criteria.
3. Create a rating system.
4. Decide to make an offer.

When you've completed this process, you can take the optional fifth step of breathing a big sigh of relief because once you and the seller have agreed on a final contract, you're in the home stretch.

Right now, though, you're in a very exciting stage of your journey to homeownership: finding your home.

Determine the Houses You Want to See

Since you and your agent will have done the work to identify your criteria, you'll be a step ahead when you begin figuring out which properties you want to see. Your agent, as a real estate professional, will have access to the local **MLS** (Multiple Listing Service). This service acts as an aggregator of available properties, and it isn't readily available to the public. The MLS will detail a property's features, its current status (such as whether it's just listed or under contract) as well as its market history. This history can help your agent by detailing just how long the house has been on the market, whether it's had previous offers that fell through or simply how many owners the home has had in its lifetime.

Using your criteria, your agent can automate search results so that you'll be alerted when property matches arrive on the market, and they'll be added to a collection in your home search app. If you see something that you'd like to check out, contact your agent and let them know. Usually, the quicker you contact them the better, especially if you're in a hot market.

Even though your agent is diligently watching the market for you, don't take your eyes off the literal and digital roads! By driving around neighborhoods where you want to live, you may be able to catch for sale or coming soon signs in front of properties that haven't hit the MLS yet or simply make your heart go pitter-patter.

For Erica Mass and her husband Dave, a little misunderstanding actually led them to discover their perfect home in Austin, Texas. After she and her Realtor had been looking for homes that matched their family's criteria in apps and through automated emails, Erica and her husband decided to go to an open house for a home that looked promising, albeit above their price range. Erica explains, "We decided we were just going to check it out to keep our options open. They were having an open house that Saturday, or so we thought.

"We showed up on Saturday right at the time the open house was supposed to start, kids in tow. Our whole family is standing on the porch as we ring the doorbell. Then, a man answers the door, barefoot and in comfy house clothes. His entire family is behind him and peeking over at us from the couch where they're watching TV. We were like, 'Hi . . . we're here for the open house?' and he replied, 'Oh, that's tomorrow.' I was mortified!

"We laughed hysterically on the way back to the car, but as we are driving out of the cul-de-sac that the not-open-house house was in, I noticed a 'Coming Soon' sign and shouted to Dave, 'Stop!'"

Erica and her husband pulled over and took a picture of the home that had caught her eye and sent photos of the "Coming Soon" sign with the Realtor's information to their agent. They were able to get a showing right away, before anyone else had put an offer on the house. After the showing, they were excited by the house and how perfectly it matched their criteria but wanted to sleep on it before they made an offer. The next morning, their agent called them and told them someone else had made an offer and advised them on how to proceed with making their offer competitive. The very next day, their offer was accepted! As Erica says, "Yay for a happy ending!"

So, whether you're driving around or searching the Internet to find potential homes, keep your eyes open and you'll be amazed at what you can find. In both of these instances, reaching out to your agent and letting them know about these options quickly can help set you up for success, especially if you're able to provide contact information available on yard signs or send links to websites.

Check Out Homes That Match Your Criteria

Nothing quite compares to exploring homes for the first time. Imagine your first day: you meet with your agent, Cindy, to review the list of homes she picked out of the MLS based on your personal criteria plus the list of properties you saw surfing the web, and then you head to the first property. Cindy opens the door, and you both step inside. What happens next is a team effort.

What You See

You've just arrived at 123 Mockingbird Lane. From your online search, you know it has three bedrooms and two baths, just like you wanted. From the sidewalk, it looks fantastic. As you step into the living room, you're immediately wowed by the fireplace and its classy stone hearth. You mentally arrange your furniture and decide your couch would fit perfectly against the side wall. As you move to the kitchen, you note that it's open and spacious, but you also wonder if there's enough counter space to do the kind of elaborate cooking you love. Walking through the bedrooms, you think they seem a little small, but the main bedroom has a great walk-in closet and a nice view of the yard. As you head back downstairs, you think you might really like it, but it's your first home to visit, so you're not quite sure.

What You See... and What Your Agent Knows

YOUR JOB is to see how the home stacks up to your wants and needs.

Questions YOU answer:

1. Does it have the right space and layout for my lifestyle?
2. Does it offer value to me?
3. Is the location convenient to my job and my kids' schools?
4. Does it have features and amenities I like?

YOUR AGENT'S JOB is to know how the home stacks up to its competition.

Questions YOUR AGENT answers:

1. Does the size and layout compare well to others around it?
2. Does it offer value in relation to other homes around it?
3. Will the location hold its value?
4. Does it show signs of major maintenance or structural concerns?

Figure 5.1

What Your Agent Knows

Having previewed the home before showing it to you, Cindy knows the fireplace is beautiful, but also knows that most of the homes in the subdivision have them. When she worked her way through the house, she looked for telltale signs of disrepair. Cindy didn't seen any stains on the ceiling, so she's thinking there haven't been any major leaks. However, she saw some slight cracks around some of the windows, and one of the doors stuck. This told her the foundation could become a problem down the road. She knows the yard is bigger than most of the ones nearby and has especially elaborate landscaping.

Comparing Notes

Above all, your home should be right for you, however offbeat and funky your tastes may be. Remember, though, that someday you will have to sell this property to someone else, and in the meantime, you'll have to deal with maintenance.

As agent Sarita Dua of Portland, Oregon, comments, "While resale value should not be the only consideration, if a home checks many of the boxes for the buyer and for many other prospective buyers, then it is a great idea to embark on an investment journey with your first home."

If your agent strongly cautions you against a particular home, we urge you to pay attention. Let's say that you decided that Mockingbird Lane was the right home for you. Most likely, Cindy would have cautioned you that foundation problems could crop up at some point and likely encouraged an inspection before you fall head over heels. Even if you don't mind a sticking door or two, the next buyer might.

At the end of the day, your relationship with your agent should be built on trust. They're your advocate and want to help you make the best decision possible. "We hope to earn a lot of trust. We like our buyers to feel taken care of each step of the way. That means our past clients and friends and family trust us with their most precious relationships," says agent Wendy Papasan. "It's an honor to serve."

It's the Big Stuff That Matters

While small repairs or renovations can add up, your major concern during your home tour is structural damage. Structural damage refers to concerns about the integrity of the building and its systems—plumbing, electrical, and more. If you have a structural concern, it could be from water damage, shifting ground, or poor construction when the house was built. Here are some things to look for:

1. Major cracks or crumbling in the foundation. (Hairline cracks are usually okay.)

2. Jagged or diagonal cracks inside the house, especially over the windows or doors.

3. Water stains on the ceiling, floors, or walls.

4. Faded, worn shingles may mean the roof needs repairing. And, if the shingles are damaged, it may mean the decking underneath is too.

5. Stains on the basement walls (or brand-new paint that may be covering stains) suggests water damage that can cause mold or structural problems. At the very least, it suggests a persistently leaky basement.

As you and your agent move into the home-viewing phase of your home-buying journey, don't be afraid to ask to look at any house that you think could be a match for your criteria. However, don't forget that you created your criteria for a reason: to help you get what you want. Your agent will be able to guide you on a well-curated search so that the homes you view are closer to your wants and you may not need to tour as many properties. As Boise, Idaho, agent April Florczyk says, "It is extremely time-consuming to look for a home. My job is to be a consultant and counsel clients through the process. If we can view fewer homes but make sure those homes truly fit what a buyer needs, they will be happier."

The adage "work smarter, not harder" applies to searching for a home, too.

Create a System: Refine as You Go

House hunting is a learning experience, and every property teaches you something. As your search progresses and your knowledge grows, tap into these new insights and continually refine your criteria. Imagine, for example, that you decided to look for homes in the Mockingbird Lane area because of its convenient location, even though the homes are a little smaller and older than you'd like. After looking at a dozen homes in the area, you realize they really are just a little too small. Maybe it's time for you to reshuffle your priorities and consider a longer commute in order to buy a bigger, newer home. These kinds of refinements are perfectly normal. In fact, they enhance your search as you share them with your agent and use them to home in on the right property for you.

Details You May Want to Consider

1. How do you like the neighborhood at different times of day?

2. Do you know what traffic is like during rush hour?

3. How will the light be at different times of day? (Will the house be too bright or too dim?)

4. How does noise carry?

5. Does the floor plan "flow," or does it have a lot of tight corners and poorly placed appliances or cabinets?

6. Is the kitchen conveniently laid out?

7. Is there enough room for storage?

8. Will your favorite furniture fit, or are you willing to replace it?

After a day or two of looking at properties, it can become hard to remember which homes were appealing, which were appalling, and why. In fact, after viewing numerous homes in a few hours, they can become one big blur. One of the best things you can do is create a system to help you rate, evaluate, and remember each home as you go. For example, San Diego, California, agent Robert Colello sits with his clients to create a rating system. Every day, Robert and his team show his clients between three to five homes, and after they visit each one, he has them rate it on a scale of one to ten, with one being the lowest score a home can receive and ten the highest.

"Based on their rating, we are either writing an offer or we're not," he says. "I tell them in my presentation that we agree that they will write an offer if the property scores above an eight. Because the reality is there are no tens. The difference between an eight and a ten is paint and carpet." So, if a house rates an eight or higher, they write an offer on the spot. This keeps his clients from being overwhelmed by what is on the market and creates a quick system by which they can accurately judge and rate a house.

A Possible System for Ranking Homes

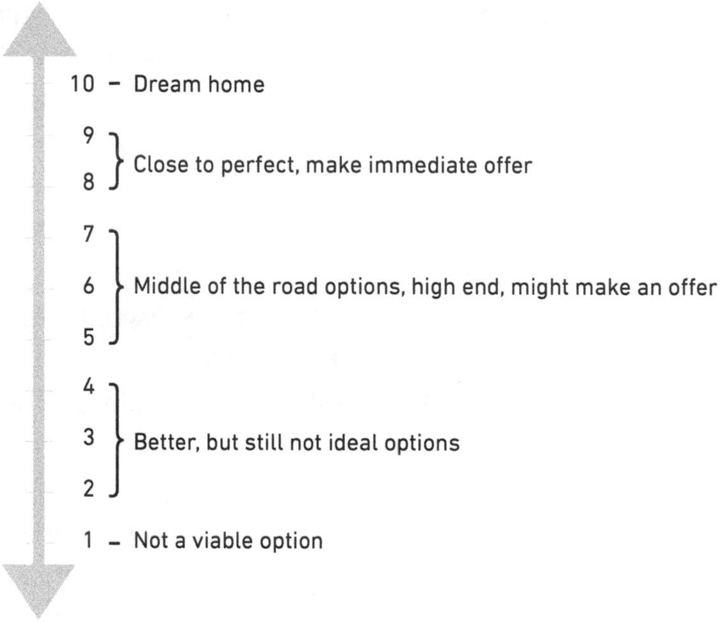

10 – Dream home

9
8 } Close to perfect, make immediate offer

7
6 } Middle of the road options, high end, might make an offer
5

4
3 } Better, but still not ideal options
2

1 – Not a viable option

Figure 5.2

Whether you follow Robert's system or create your own, we suggest you have some way to take notes as you go: use an app on your phone, take photos, or even bring good old-fashioned pen and paper with you to help you remember each home distinctly. Write down the address of each property you visit before you get out of the car. While you tour the home, take short notes about the things you like and don't like (including any areas of concern), and note any distinguishing features (for example, a purple birdhouse or a stained-glass window) that will jog your memory after a long period of looking. And don't forget to snap some photos! Whipping out your smartphone to take pictures of the property is a great way to track the homes you've visited.

At the end of the tour, you can revisit your notes and

rank the properties according to affordability, size, features, amenities, condition, layout, and location, among other things. After you do this a few times, it'll become easier to figure out which homes don't fit your needs and which ones do. It'll also be clear if you've got any nonnegotiables that can help simplify the process even further. "When we are touring a home, if there's something that the buyer has identified as a must-have and it's not there, I'll point that out right away," Nashville, Tennessee, agent Alex Helton says. "I also try to keep the focus on two or three homes; otherwise, everything can start to blur."

Sight Unseen

In some markets and for some homes, you need to be prepared to move faster than the pace we are describing. If the market is hot or you have to relocate quickly, like can happen when in the military, you may have to make an offer on a house sight unseen or via virtual walk-through only. If the home search is indeed a little like going on a date, this would be speed dating with the help of a trusted matchmaker.

Review your notes on each home. What are the pros and cons? Does the house fall in the range for making an offer? Or do you need to keep searching? If you've got yourself a winner—it's time to get serious about making an offer, which we'll cover in the next chapter.

Notes to Take Home

- Keep your eyes open and your agent in the loop as you look for listings.

- Look for structural integrity, instead of being distracted by surface-level appearances.

- You'll learn as you look at homes—so you should refine your priorities along the way.

- Keep notes and take pictures; this will help you keep houses and their features fresh in your mind later when you are making decisions.

- Visit *YourFirstHomeBook.com* for worksheets and other helpful resources.

JAY PAPASAN'S FIRST HOME

When we lived in New York City, it never occurred to us to buy a home—almost everybody we knew rented. Then, we moved to Austin, Texas, where I started working for Keller Williams. Mo Anderson, our CEO at the time, taught an orientation class on balance sheets, assets, and liabilities. She was passionate about our building financial independence and growing our net worth. Her advice sunk in. Suddenly, not buying a home just wasn't an option.

While it didn't happen overnight, we got to work immediately. My wife, Wendy, and I started paying off our college debt and saving money for a down payment. And once we began looking, it happened fast. People have always told me that when you find the right house,

---

* *Photograph courtesy of the Papasan family.*

you will know right away—kind of like meeting the right person and falling in love.

When we first saw the house pictured on the Internet, it didn't look at all promising. The black-and-white photograph, which had been taken through a metal chain-link fence in terrible lighting, made the house look dejected and sad. Still, it had the right address—in South Austin, near Zilker Park and Barton Springs. It was the classic Austin neighborhood. And the price was right too, only $5,000 more than we had budgeted.

The house looked even worse in person than in the photograph. Pink cinder block masquerading as stucco. No real driveway, just broken concrete and gravel. And that ugly chain-link fence guarding an overgrown lawn. To make matters worse, it was raining that day. But when we opened the front door and went inside, I remember saying to Wendy, "This is it."

That little bungalow had everything we valued: location, layout, and light. The previous owners had added a nice living space at the back with lots of windows. We immediately began referring to it as "the sunroom."

Even though I knew this house was the one for us, we forced ourselves to look at four others that day. But by 9:45 in the evening, we called our real estate agent and put in an offer. We bought it for $175,000.

Wendy's dad is a great handyman, and she's pretty handy, too. He helped us install a new kitchen sink and garbage disposal. Wendy and I painted the house in bright pastel colors and put in a stone walkway and new floors. We ripped up the chain-link fence, except for the gate with the little metal lions on top, which became the focal point of our landscaping. My grandmother in

Mississippi was known as "The Gardener." She gave us daylilies and hollyhocks to plant. Before long, that little pink bungalow looked quite charming.

When I think of that first home, it reminds me of a carefree time with lots of dinner parties and hanging out with friends in the backyard. We have great memories of working on the improvements together. We spent three very happy years there until Gus, our first child, came along and we needed to find something larger.

We still have that house and use it as a rental property. Wendy enjoys showing it to prospective renters. She says it's easy to sell something you really love. The best part? That funny little house we bought for $175,000 appreciated to be worth more than $325,000 in only five years.

Although we didn't really plan it that way, it's turned out to be a great investment. As Wendy says, "It's the best investment we didn't know we were making."

Jay Papasan is vice president of strategic content at Keller Williams Realty.

CHAPTER 6

MAKE AN OFFER

"I started talking with my client Merina a couple years ago about purchasing a home, after she'd graduated college and landed a good job. She contacted me a few months ago about her desire to do just that," recalls agent Josh Stern of Salt Lake City, Utah. However, a hot market meant that there weren't a lot of quality homes that matched Merina's needs and wants. "I had to show her homes that had already sold in the past thirty days that fit her criteria, because the active properties that were in her area or price range were still active for a reason—they weren't good properties at their prices."

After discussing their options and going through a number of properties, Merina and Josh finally found three homes that matched her criteria—but all three already had offers on them because of the competitive market. "The first two we couldn't win. The third house, however, chose our offer. Not because we were the highest offer, but because we had agreed to let the seller live in the property after closing for thirty days at *no charge*," Josh says. "The seller was an older lady who needed some time to move to her next property. And, while our offer wasn't the highest, it met the needs of both buyer and seller. Merina was ecstatic."

Josh's story illustrates two general truths about shopping for homes. First, it's important to remember not everything is about price. Sometimes, winning with a seller means landing on the right terms. When you find a home you love, it's important to step back and make sure that when you make an offer, it's one that's a win-win for everyone. Second, if your offer on a property doesn't win, there will be another opportunity.

Write a Strong Offer

When you were searching for your dream home, you were just that—a dreamer. You needed to be romantic, listen to your emotions, let yourself fall in love. But writing an offer requires putting on a different hat. You need to approach this process with a cool head. Remove those rose-colored glasses, and adopt a realistic perspective about your market. No matter the market, there are three basic components of any offer: price, terms, and contingencies (or "conditions" in Canada).

The Three Components of an Offer

1. Price

2. Terms

3. Contingencies

1. Price

Most things we buy have a fixed price that is nonnegotiable. You can't usually walk into a department store and convince the person behind the counter to sell you a frying pan for less than sticker price. But prices on homes, much like cars, function differently. You can negotiate on the price, which is part of the fun of buying a home.

That being said, one of the most common misconceptions buyers have about the home-buying process is thinking they're supposed to submit an offer that is below list price and then haggle to meet in the middle. In slow markets, this is a strategy that can work in your favor, but in fast ones, it can get you into trouble. Agent Jennifer Barnes once worked with a very successful young businessman who was determined to find a deal. To him that meant paying well below list price. In his search to find a deal, though, he found a home he truly loved. He lowballed anyway, offering $120,000 under the $795,000 asking price. The sellers rejected his offer—and refused to deal with him again.

"That house was on the market for eight months after that, but they would not sell it to him," Jennifer says. "That's the risk you run when you lowball. You can personally affront the sellers, so they just don't care that your money's green." Making a good offer is less about lowballing and more about compromise. And it requires understanding how homes are priced to begin with.

The right price fairly reflects the market value of the home you want to buy. To find this price, your agent will pull together a **competitive market analysis (CMA)**, which is a set of recently sold homes that resemble the one you want in size, condition, location, and amenities. These records are also called "comparables" or "**comps**." You'll get the best market insights from the homes most similar to the one you're looking for. The perfect comp would be one that's identical to your dream home, situated next door, and that sold this morning. Perfect comps like that are harder to find than a black cat in a coal mine, though, which is why writing a competitive offer is more of an art than a science.

Your set of comps will enable you to determine an average cost per square foot, which forms the basis of a competitive offer. For example, imagine that on average, three-bedroom homes in Oak Knoll sold for about $130 per square foot last month. The nicer homes sold for around $135 per square foot, while those that needed a little work went for about $115. You need to decide where the home you want fits into that range. Does it need some updates? Is it located on one of the busier streets in the neighborhood? In that case, a fair price would probably be on the lower end. On the other hand, if it has an extra bathroom, a finished basement, or has been spectacularly maintained, you should probably offer a little more.

Understanding Pricing

Welcome to the Grasslands, a quiet neighborhood built in the 1960s. Most homes here have three bedrooms, range in size from 1,500 to 1,750 square feet, and have been selling between $200,000 and $250,000. You want to make an offer on 345 Cardinal Lane. What should your offer be?

123 Eagle Pass

Three bedrooms
1.5 baths
1,550 sq feet
No recent updates

**Sold last week for
$129/sq foot, or
$200,000**

345 Cardinal Lane

Three bedrooms
2 baths
1,650 sq feet
Modest updates

**You offer
$136/sq foot, or
$225,000**

223 Robin Lane

Three bedrooms
2.5 baths
1,725 sq feet
Luxury updates

**Sold last week for
$145/sq foot, or
$250,000**

Figure 6.1

In either situation, we're talking above or below *average*, not necessarily above or below what the seller is asking. Smart sellers go through a similar process of comparison to price their homes fairly. If your math and the seller's figures work out the same, you may very well offer close to list price. But, if your analysis reveals that a property is indeed overpriced, go ahead and offer less.

First-time home buyer Melissa Robertson and her husband looked for their first home for around three months. But because they wanted a one-story home in a specific part of Austin, their options were limited. "We toured six or seven homes," she says. "We put an offer on one but got outbid. The house we bought was the second one we bid on. While it was about $25,000 overpriced, it was in a popular area, so the price was justified and still within our budget. Our agent advised us on what a good price was that worked within our budget but that was fair and reasonable for the seller."

As this story demonstrates, it's always important to factor in market realities. The important thing is figuring out what *type* of market you're in.

Buyers' Market vs. Sellers' Market

Depending on when you're buying a home, you could find yourself in either a buyers' or a sellers' market—and those two markets directly impact your home-buying process. A buyers' market is when the supply outstrips the demand. That is to say, there are more houses on the market than there are people looking to buy. In this instance, as a buyer you have more leeway when it comes to negotiating prices because you have more options.

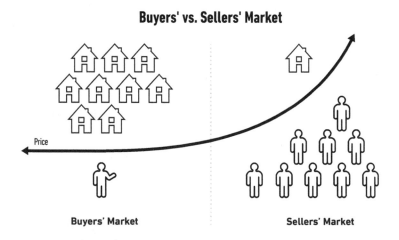

Buyers' vs. Sellers' Market

Price

Buyers' Market   Sellers' Market

Figure 6.2

A sellers' market, by contrast, is when there's more demand than there is supply. In this case, there are more people looking to buy a house than there are homes available to purchase. This gives the seller an edge, because they'll often end up with the prospect of multiple offers on their home. In these types of markets, you may have to put in multiple offers, spend more time negotiating offers, and be more accommodating with the offers you do make.

How Buyers Can Win with Sellers in a Competitive Market

If you find yourself in a seriously competitive sellers-based market, there are some things you can do to help ensure your offer is taken more seriously.

- **Pay in Cash:** Paying in cash isn't an easy ask and it isn't always feasible for everyone. However, if you can manage to make a cash offer for a home, most sellers will have a hard time saying no. Because you don't have to hassle with finding a mortgage, it'll expedite the closing process; it also means instant cash in the seller's pocket. But coming up with that kind of cash can be hard for first-time home buyers. This is where having someone—say a parent—to help you finance might be useful. Or, in many areas, there are some businesses that will provide the cash and let you pay them in "rent" until you are able to find a mortgage. Ask your agent if they have a service they can recommend.

- **A Little Extra Time:** Like the older woman in Merina's story, sometimes the best way to get your offer taken seriously is to figure out what the seller needs, and often what they need is a little extra time in the house to get their affairs in order. That could mean working out a deal, like Merina did, where the seller stays in the house an additional thirty days for free, or participating in a leaseback program, where they pay you rent for staying on the property for a set period of time.

- **Go Big or Go Home:** The truth is in extreme markets you may need to take extreme measures in order to make an offer stick. That could mean offering listing price or higher, forgoing repairs, and more. The trick is figuring out what the seller wants and making sure your offer works to meet those needs.

If you're facing a multiple-offer situation and you really love the property, you may decide to offer a little more than you would in a less-competitive market. A few thousand dollars may be a small price to pay to make sure your offer is accepted. "Sometimes people get so caught up in making a low offer they lose the house they really want," says agent Linda McKissack of Dallas, Texas. "I hate to see people so disappointed when $5,000 would have made all the difference."

A sellers' market also means you need to be more decisive and action oriented when it comes to picking a home and making an offer, or you might end up in a multiple-offer scenario. Had Steve and Denise from Austin, Texas, not acted decisively, such a multiple-offer scenario might have unfolded for them. They were engaged and decided to buy a home Steve would move into before the wedding. When their agent, Gary Keller, took them to their first home, it was love at first sight. But then, Denise squeezed Steve's elbow and said, "And just think, this is the first one we've seen."

While shopping around might've been beneficial or useful in a buyers' market, Steve and Denise were on a tight budget in a sellers' market, which put them at an immediate disadvantage. Gary knew that if they loved this house and it fit their budget, they needed to make an offer quickly or they'd likely lose the home. After sitting and discussing their options with them, he was able to convince the couple to go ahead and make an offer.

They agreed on a price, presented the offer, and the house was theirs. For years, Gary, Steve, and Denise reminisced about the experience. They were proud of their smart and courageous decision to buy it on the spot. And they agreed it wouldn't have been possible if Gary hadn't helped them be so clear about their priorities.

Making Multiple Offers

If you find yourself in a hot market with multiple homes you like, it may be in your best interest to just go ahead and make multiple offers. While that may seem like a big deal (you don't want to be on the hook for three houses) the reality is making an offer doesn't make you obligated to buy that house, even if it is accepted. It's simply an offer. Nothing is set in stone at this part in the process. If you have more questions, just be sure to talk to your agent.

---

2. Terms

There's a lot more to real estate offers than price. You and the seller have to agree on many details, such as when the deal will close, whether the seller will keep any of the décor (such as window treatments or appliances), and who pays for **closing costs**. (Though, in Canada, the buyers always pay the closing costs.) These factors are called "**terms**," and they give buyers and sellers additional flexibility in crafting a winning deal. When it comes to terms, remember that everything is negotiable. However, different markets have informal rules governing the kinds of requests you can make of sellers. Your agent will let you know what the seller will probably expect, as well as the pros and cons of deviating from market norms. The six basic terms in a real estate offer are: schedule, conveyances, commissions, closing costs, home warranty, and earnest money.

Schedule

As a first-time buyer, you'll have to fit closing day around moving, jobs, school, *The Bachelor* finale, the end of your lease, and the expiration date on your loan preapproval. The seller has it even worse, simultaneously selling an old house and buying a new one. To help keep everyone focused, your contract establishes a schedule for the events that have to happen before closing. If your agent writes it well, it will keep things flowing smoothly for both you and the seller. In most contracts, the major milestones are:

- *Response time* (or "irrevocable clause" in Canada): This is the period in which the seller must respond to your offer. It is usually no more than a few days.
- *Subject-to or contingency clauses*: These are clauses that prevent a contract from becoming binding and protect the buyer until the property is inspected, the title is searched, and financing is approved. The general clauses are the subject-to-inspection clause, the subject-to-marketable title clause, and the subject-to-financing clause. That way, if your property inspection reveals that unsuspected, major repairs are needed or if you cannot obtain financing, then these clauses allow you to walk away from the deal. These contingency clauses are discussed in more detail later in this chapter.

- *Expiration date* (or "requisition date" in Canada): This is the day before which the deal must be closed. It's usually thirty to sixty days after the contract is accepted. If you or the seller don't have everything ready to close before the expiration date, it is possible to extend the contract. However, both buyer and seller must accept the extension, so delays can kill the deal.
- *Closing date* (or "completion date" in Canada): Closing date is the day that the property officially changes hands between the buyer and the seller. The seller is paid by the buyer, and in exchange the title is transferred to the buyer.
- *Occupancy date* (or "possession date" in Canada): This is when you can move into your home. Generally, buyers want to take occupancy on closing day (or the next day, when the funds have officially cleared). Sellers, on the other hand, often want the option of staying in the house after closing because it gives them more flexibility in arranging their home purchase. Because of liability issues, however, most agents recommend against allowing sellers to lease back.

Should I Let the Seller Lease Back?

Sometimes sellers offer to pay rent on their house so they can stay in it after closing. This is called a "leaseback." A lease-back helps sellers coordinate moves or gives them certainty their old house is sold before they go under contract with the house they're buying. This kind of arrangement can have some risks. It can lead to possible future repairs, possible delays in moving, and more. But that doesn't mean you should discount the notion altogether. If you're in a sellers' market, for instance, allowing sellers to stay on for a longer time might help you clinch the deal. Just be smart, talk with your agent, and make sure any agreement is explicitly written out formally in your offer and contract. That way, both parties will have legal protection.

Conveyances

Conveyances are the items that stay with the house when the sellers leave. In general, anything not permanently attached to the home is considered personal property, which goes with the seller. Real property, or fixtures, stay. But what about those beautiful blinds that fit the picture window so perfectly? What about that expensive stainless-steel fridge or the antique chandelier in the dining room?

The standard contract forms used in your area may spell out which items typically convey in your area. And the seller's disclosure oftentimes states what items the seller wants to keep. However, everything is negotiable. If you want something that isn't a wall, a roof, or a floor, and it's not already mentioned in the contract, you may want to add it to the forms. For instance, maybe the chandelier in the dining room is a must-have, or you'd like to keep the seller's tractor because it's a rural property. Bring it up with your agent, and they can broach the subject with the seller's agent. Maybe they'll be happy to leave it for free or will accept leaving you that tractor in exchange for a set amount of money or in lieu of a repair.

Sellers, however, can always say no. The trick is to negotiate, not make demands. And, if you have any doubts about something that comes with the house, the best course of action is to simply discuss—convey your wishes and go from there.

Commission

The real estate **commission**, or fee, for both the agent who works with the seller and the agent who works with the buyer. The commission is usually paid for out of the sales price by the seller unless you, as the buyer, have arranged to pay the agent you work with separately.

Closing Costs

Buyers nearly always pay their own closing costs. However, if you're short on cash and want the seller to either pay closing costs outright (which is rare) or help you roll them into your loan (which is more common), you need to write that into your contract.

Home Warranty

In many areas, sellers often provide a one-year **home warranty**. Home warranties are different from home-owner's insurance, which can protect you from massive, unexpected tragedies like fires or break-ins. Warranties, on the other hand, cover repairs or replacement of appliances and major systems, such as the roof, plumbing, siding, or wiring. Read the warranty carefully to make sure that everything you want covered is included. If you wait until later to add new items, you'll probably have to get the home professionally inspected all over again, as warranty companies don't want you to wait for something to break before deciding to cover it.

Earnest Money

Earnest money, or a deposit, protects the seller from the possibility of you unexpectedly pulling out of the deal. If you're in a hot market, a large deposit can convince the seller you're, well, *earnest* about making the deal work. Earnest money is usually a percentage of the price of the property; it goes into an escrow account and becomes part of your down payment at closing. If the deal never reaches closing due to an error, omission, or decision on your part, you'll likely lose the deposit. (In Canada, earnest money is deposited in a real estate trust account. Buyers who opt out of a deal may face greater liability than those in the United States. Check with your agent for details.)

3. Contingencies

Imagine you go under contract, and two days before closing, the seller leaves a candle burning and starts a fire that destroys half the house. Do you still want to buy the property according to the price and terms of your initial contract? Of course not. This is why most contracts include what are known as conditions or contingency clauses—they let you out of the deal if the house has a problem that didn't exist, or about which you weren't aware, when you went under contract. Again, standard contractual language varies from place to place, so when you're writing your contract, be sure to talk to your agent about which clauses are already included and which your agent will have to write in on your behalf. Here are a few of the common contingencies for most real estate contracts:

Inspections

An inspection contingency protects you from paying too much for a home that's hiding major problems. For example, imagine you went under contract to buy a house for $335,000, but a week later a property inspection (explained in Chapter 7) revealed that its sparkling appearance was hiding out-of-date wiring, nonfunctioning plumbing, and an infestation of gremlins that were allowed to snack after midnight. Do you still want to pay $335,000? Do you even want to buy it at all? An inspection contingency enables you to renegotiate or walk away.

Financing

At its most basic, a financing contingency lets you out of the contract in the event that you can't qualify for a mortgage. In addition, it keeps you from being forced to accept an unfavorable mortgage if your loan paperwork comes in with a higher interest rate than you were promised. For example, a financing contingency might say that the contract is subject to your acquiring "a $350,000 mortgage for a term of thirty years at a rate of no higher than 4 percent." If the only loan you can find is at 5 percent, you can legally walk away from the contract, and for good reason. While one or even a half-percent might not seem like a big deal, it could be the difference between a budget that invites the occasional night on the town or a lot of Saturdays at home with frozen pizza.

Appraisal

In some states, an appraisal contingency is a requirement. An appraisal contingency guarantees that a home will be professionally appraised, and you will only purchase it if the value of the appraisal is at least as much as what you've agreed to pay for the home. In essence, this contingency protects you from overpaying for a home that is appraised for less than what you've agreed to pay for it and protects the lender from giving out a bigger loan than is necessary for the value of the home. Depending on the state, this can often be attached to the financing contingency. But that isn't the case everywhere, so make sure to check with your agent. As always, they'll keep you apprised of the situation.

Clear Title

Just as some properties are hiding physical flaws, some homes are hiding legal flaws. A clear title contingency releases you from having to buy a home whose ownership is uncertain or that's subject to a lien to pay off the seller's debts. The issue of title is explained in Chapter 7.

Insurance

Is your ideal home in an area prone to flooding or other natural disasters? Then it's possible that you may be required to provide proof of hazard insurance. If it turns out your home is uninsurable, meaning it's too hazard prone to qualify for insurance, this allows you to bail out of the deal and walk away safely.

Condition at Delivery

Houses, like babies, are "delivered." A good contract will require that the seller deliver the house vacant and in good condition—no pizza boxes, no old newspapers. This prevents a stressed-out seller from leaving trash or old furniture they don't feel like moving. This clause is also what protects you in case something drastic happens to the home (such as a fire) before closing.

Community Restrictions

Many homes (particularly in new-home developments) are in neighborhoods that require membership in a homeowner's association. Consider including a contingency that lets you review and agree to the CC&Rs and which will allow you to pull out of the deal if you don't like what you see. For example, the association fees are too high or the neighborhood has rules you reject—then you don't have to go through with the purchase of the home.

Reaching Agreement

Once you and your agent have written a contract, your agent will submit it to the seller's agent. If you've written a great offer, the seller might accept it on the spot. Otherwise, it's time to start negotiating. The seller may write a counteroffer that, for example, asks for an earlier closing date and a slightly higher price. Then the ball's back in your court to decide whether to accept their changes or to counter their counter.

If the idea of negotiating makes you nervous, don't worry—you won't negotiate directly with the seller. Instead, your agent will do all the talking with the seller's agent, providing a buffer between you and the seller and saving you the stress of in-person negotiations. Remember, negotiating skills were one of the main qualities you looked for when you hired your agent, and this is when the great ones get another chance to excel.

Letters with Offers

There are a million stories out there about how "love letters" from buyers to sellers have sealed the deal. Love letters, or offer letters, have been used throughout the years as a means of appealing to the seller in a competitive market. However, while many people still try to use these letters to give their offer an edge, they can (intentionally or otherwise) lead to discriminatory housing practices.

In 1968, the United States government passed what is known as the Fair Housing Act. This act ensures that no renter or buyer could be discriminated against by race, religion, sex, national origin, family, or disability status. This law was largely drafted as a part of the larger Civil Rights movement at the time in order to get rid of discriminatory housing practices. It helps clamp down on things like red lining or unfair lending practices.

While writing a letter to someone you want to buy a home from may seem harmless, the reality is it can easily violate this law. By disclosing who you are, your family status, or any other personal details—you could be unintentionally appealing to any bias a seller has. We here at Keller Williams think housing and generational wealth are rights that everyone should have equal access to. So, no matter how well intentioned you may be, we encourage you avoid buyer "love letters" in an effort to create a happier, more equitable world for everyone.

When you and the seller reach an agreement and both parties sign the contract, that check you wrote as earnest money will be deposited into an escrow account. When that happens, you've passed another major, exciting milestone on the path to homeownership.

Navigating the Ups and Downs

Now, before you move on, there's a lot that can happen between the moment you decide to put an offer on a home and the day you get the keys. Depending on the market you're in, finding the home for you can be as easy as walking through the front door or as hard as, well, walking through fifty front doors. Woof, I am tired just *thinking* about walking through that many doors.

For instance, if you find yourself in a shifting or hot market, the road to finding the right home may be a bit more of a challenge. For first-time buyers April and Valerie, it took ten attempts before they closed on their home. "We got engaged on a Saturday and started looking at houses the following Monday," Valerie says. "And by the end of that week, the country and Austin were in a tailspin because of COVID-19." Their agent, Chris Hall, worked with them closely, navigating the uncertain market and helping them clarify what they wanted and needed in a home so that they could make quick offers. "Chris took time to explain why each offer was rejected so that we could make our next offer stronger," April adds. "He was able to advise us to start making more competitive offers with different incentives like additional money and shorter closing times. In the end, we were able to make an offer within hours of touring a great home—and we got it!"

Like April and Valerie, you may end up finding yourself with rejected offers. You may have difficulty finding a home that you like or have negotiations fall through on an offer in progress. But the important thing is to not get discouraged. "My mom kept telling us that the house we would end up getting would be the house that was meant for us, and while we kind of groaned about her advice at the time, it ended up being the case. When our tenth offer was accepted, it was on a house that we absolutely loved," April says.

Your journey to homeownership isn't going to be like anyone else's, and that's okay! There may be ups and downs and twists and turns in the road, but in the end, you'll find a home that you'll be able to make memories in for years to come.

Notes to Take Home

You now know and understand the three basic components of a purchase offer: price, terms, and contingencies.

- Price—the right price to offer must fairly reflect the true market value of the home you want to buy. Your agent's market research will guide this decision.

- Terms—the other financial and timing factors that will be included in the offer. Terms fall under six basic categories in a real estate offer:

    - Schedule—a schedule of events that has to happen before closing.

    - Conveyances—the items that stay with the house when the seller leaves.

    - Commission—the real estate commission, or fee, for both the agent who works with the seller and the agent who works with the buyer.

- Closing costs—it's standard for buyers to pay for their closing costs, but if you want to roll the costs into the loan, you need to write that into the contract.

- Home warranty—this covers repairs or replacement of appliances and major systems, such as the roof, plumbing, siding, or wiring. You may ask the seller to pay for this.

- Earnest money—this protects the seller from the possibility of you unexpectedly pulling out of the deal. It makes a statement about the seriousness of your offer.

- Contingencies (or conditions)—these clauses let you out of the deal if the house has a problem that didn't exist, or about which you weren't aware, when you went under contract. They specify any event that will need to take place in order for you to fulfill the contract.

- Visit *YourFirstHomeBook.com* for worksheets and other helpful resources.

JP LEWIS' FIRST HOME

When I was growing up, my parents owned a nice-sized lime green brick home in a neighborhood in South Texas. I was fortunate that it was a very stable environment and they lived there for 42 years, before moving recently to be closer to their grandchildren. When I think about my childhood home, I think about the massive holidays my entire extended family spent celebrating there—my dad and uncles hanging out in the garage, lots of cousins running around, and my mom and aunts making everything perfect for us.

I knew owning a home was something I wanted to do, but it wasn't until I was in my twenties that I started to recognize how important homeownership was for changing our wealth trajectory. It was around this time that I started listening to some key mentors in my life

---

* Photograph courtesy of the Lewis family.

and realized I wanted to purchase a house with the goal of building wealth for myself and, in the process, improving the legacy of my family.

I started saving for a down payment and looking for a home for about a year before I found the right place. I knew I wanted to find something that allowed me to rent out part of it to help pay down part of my mortgage. I started the search process looking for duplexes, thanks to a mentor's advice, but found a place with a separate mother-in-law suite that hit all the criteria I was looking for. At $199,000, 3100 Fontana Drive had a unit with three bedrooms and one bathroom in the front and a one-bedroom and one-bath unit in the back, with a shared wall between them. Built in 1957, it needed some work, but I was willing to put in the sweat equity to make it my own. Even better, it was located right across the street from a local university, which I knew would be a good source of potential roommates.

Although the entire place was mine, I chose to sacrifice and took the significantly smaller, less updated portion of the house. Although it wasn't as nice, doing so enabled me to fill the front of the house with multiple renters. Lucky for me, they covered 70–80 percent of my mortgage payment each month. I was living in a prime location, in a home that I owned, and yet I was only paying $300 a month of my own mortgage. To me, this was a dream scenario.

When I bought 3100 Fontana Drive, I realized I was opening a door to building more wealth for myself than I had once thought possible. While I did have naysayers who were, at first, disappointed in my choice of house, I understood the future potential this home had. I did my homework and knew I wanted to capitalize on the opportunity the house presented based on the market we were in. And during the one year I lived in the back apartment of that home, I was able to save up enough money for another down payment for a second property I soon purchased.

I still own 3100 Fontana Drive as an investment property. Over the years, it's appreciated in value to between $600,000 and $700,000, and we're currently developing plans to tear it down and put two new units on the same lot. That home taught me the importance of surrounding yourself with people who understand homeownership and taking the time to learn the value of real estate as a wealth-building tool. It's because of the advice of the people I surrounded myself with in my early twenties that I became a real estate investor, and I am so thankful that they taught me what it means to own something that will grow in value.

JP Lewis is the vice president of Keller Williams Worldwide.

CHAPTER 7

PERFORM DUE DILIGENCE

Tonja Pitzer of Tulsa, Oklahoma, fell in love with a 1920s home that had a big, beautiful front porch. She quickly put it under contract and ordered her inspection. The report, however, wasn't pretty. There were termite problems. Gutters were falling down. The garage was keeling over. The entire home had antiquated knob-and-tube wiring. And, she discovered, the porch provided an even bigger surprise.

"There were only a few bricks keeping it up," she says. "The ground underneath the porch was wearing away, so every few years the owners would stuff another brick underneath the post to hold it up."

Rather than negotiating extensive repairs, Pitzer decided to walk away from the sale. "I loved that house and hated to let it go," she says. "But with all those problems, it didn't make sense to buy it."

Sometimes, no matter how much we love a house, the best call is not to buy it. Of course, this can often be a hard decision to make. After investing so much time looking for houses, you can feel heartbroken at the idea of letting it go. Adding insult to injury, you also have to pay for the very inspection that made it clear you needed to walk away. All in all, it can end up making you feel like your time and money have been wasted.

The fact is inspections and the costs associated with them aren't a waste of anything. Unlike most major purchases, once you buy a home, you can't return it if something breaks or doesn't quite work like it's supposed to. That's why things like property inspections are so valuable—for a relatively small investment, they can save a fortune in time and money.

When it comes to the homestretch of buying your first home, two things become incredibly important: getting your home inspected and getting your home insured. These steps tend to go hand in hand, as many companies require some type of inspection in order to insure your house. They're also important for ensuring you're getting the value you're paying for and protecting it.

Property Inspection

Generally, you should be shopping for a home inspector and home insurance at the same time. A home includes dozens of systems and features, all designed to make our lives comfortable and pleasant, but all of which can cause serious headaches if they malfunction. An inspection exposes your dream home's hidden flaws, so you can go back to the seller to negotiate before you become the owner. Typically, sellers will either agree to fix the problems or reduce the sales price to cover the cost of fixing them. "A home inspection is like getting an annual physical," says D.C. agent James Williams. "It tells you the general health of the house and gives you an idea of the minor and major issues of the home. An experienced agent can help the buyer decide if these issues are cosmetic in nature or something they should walk away from. We like to recommend that the buyers purchase a home warranty for peace of mind."

Before you hire your own inspector, we encourage you to carefully review the **seller's disclosure** (known as a "seller's property information sheet" in Canada), a written statement of the owners' knowledge of the property's current condition. Your agent will get the disclosure from the seller's agent. The requirements for what exactly must be shared in a seller's disclosure vary state by state, but they usually must include any information about large repairs or structural issues. For example, you may be considering a property that another buyer previously had under contract but had pulled out when the buyer's inspector found a major crack in the foundation. The seller would have to include that information in the disclosure, giving you the opportunity to walk away (if you wanted to) before springing for another inspection.

Working with an Inspector

The information your inspector provides will be critical to making a well-informed home-buying decision. Unlike when you searched for pictures of that weird mole under your arm, you don't want to just go with the first result that pops up in your web search—you want to make a smart choice. Your agent should be able to give you a referral to a trusted professional. As you are moving forward with the inspector, keep the following questions in mind:

1. Do They Have Errors and Omission Insurance?

This insurance protects inspectors—and you—if they make a mistake in their inspection report that leads you to buy a flawed home.

2. Do They Specialize in a Certain Kind of Construction?

Properties often have quirks related to their age, location, or construction style and some inspectors have gained particular insight into these traits. Working in Long Beach, California, agent Shannon Jones says she sees many homes with foundation troubles because of the particular kind of beach sand used in their construction. So, when one of her clients is considering a home with that sort of foundation, she steers the person toward an expert who knows exactly what to inspect. Brand-new homes also have quirks that call for a specialist. We don't want you to be unduly stressed; your agent can help you decide whether your home needs a specialized inspector.

3. What Does It Cost?

Inspections can cost as little as $200 or more than $1,000, and you (the buyer) will be responsible for that cost whether you end up buying the property or not. As of 2020, the national average was $337 for a home inspection. Generally speaking, the price of an inspection is determined by several factors. First, some inspectors charge more—a higher price may indicate higher quality. Second, larger homes and those with more bathrooms and air-conditioning units cost more because they require more work.

However, Debbie Abadie, a Houston, Texas, agent who is also a licensed inspector, warns buyers to avoid inspectors who base their quotes on the price of the home. It takes about the same amount of work to inspect a 2,000-square-foot home with two bathrooms, whether the sales price is $200,000 or half a million. "If the inspector asks how much you're paying for the house, hang up as fast as you can," she says.

4. How Soon Are They Available?

The results of an inspection may launch you into negotiations and repairs that must be completed before closing, so it's important to schedule an inspection (at a time you can attend) as quickly as possible. If you're in a competitive market, you may also find that inspectors can be booked out and difficult to pin down. Either way, your agent will help you get the inspector and the inspection you need.

New Houses Need Inspection Too

Don't think that you can skip the inspection just because you're buying a brand-new home. In fact, flaws in new construction can be even harder to spot than in older homes because their symptoms haven't had a chance to show up yet. Buyer Teresa Van Horn, for example, didn't discover for months that a slow leak from an improperly welded pipe was rotting out the bathroom wall of her new condo. When her condo was inspected, the pipe was already hidden behind the pristine, white wall.

If you're buying a new home, find an inspector who is experienced with new construction. Some agents suggest buyers go one step further and have the builder's work inspected during the construction after big milestones are complete, like after the wiring and plumbing are installed but before the drywall covers them up. If you can handle the additional expense, you may be able to catch a mistake before it's too far along.

What to Expect When You're Inspecting

No matter how busy you are, you should attend your inspection in person. It's your chance to get a professional introduction to the fuse box, air-conditioning system, water heater, and other systems you may soon own. Plus, inspectors aren't required to move furniture or look under carpets, so it's possible for even good inspectors to miss things. "Inspections are supremely important," says agent Josh Stern. "We let our clients know quite often that they're going to get a bible-sized list of potential problems from the inspector but not to be alarmed. Our focus is on *major* deferred maintenance, safety concerns, and systems failures."

While you probably don't want to move furniture around to see what the seller is hiding—imagine the liability if you knocked over their entertainment center in your quest to look behind it—you can certainly flip back a throw rug to see if it's covering cracked tiles or peek under the sink to see if there's evidence of a leak. And, in the end, an extra set of eyes can only help.

Most general inspectors inspect the house from the foundation to the roof. This includes a myriad of things: plumbing, electrical systems, heating, ventilation, windows and doors, the drainage system, and much more. For other properties, like condos, some exterior items might not always be included in the inspection because they are cared for by whomever manages the property. It's the inspector's job to check as much of the property as possible without risking injury. However, it's important to remember that inspectors can't see everything in a house—they can't peel back walls or floors to see what's behind or underneath. So, make sure to keep an eye out for problems, no matter how clean the inspection may seem.

After the inspection, you and your agent will get the inspection report sent to you either digitally or through the mail within three to four days. At this point, you can both sit and review what the inspection turned up. Different inspectors give reports in different ways, some with a system of quick words like "serviceable" or "needs to be replaced," while others give write-ups that are more in-depth. Many will also include photos of what the inspector saw while checking various parts of the property. Set aside some time to go over all of this information, by yourself and with your agent. If you have any questions, make sure that you either broach them with your agent or reach out to the inspector to get clarification. From there, you can begin to put together a list of things that need to be fixed and start negotiating with the seller.

Repairs and Renegotiation

While it may seem like an inspection report is something to skip over or skim, we really do urge you to take the time to thoroughly read it. Many agents say they're amazed by the number of people who approach their inspection like a hurdle to jump over, rather than as a valuable new source of information about the property they're considering buying.

"When my daughter bought her house, she didn't pay attention to the details of her inspection and ended up with all sorts of problems," says one New York agent. "This is all too common. In the rush of things, people don't take time to read the report and miss the opportunity to make the seller take care of problems for them."

Even a dream home comes with a few problems. If you find yourself feeling increasingly nervous as you read through your home inspection report—don't panic. There are no perfect homes. Unless your home is new, it's virtually guaranteed to have some wear and tear. An inspector's job is to note everything that's not perfect about the property, right down to the minor, easily fixed problems, such as replacing missing window screens or broken light switch plates.

However, even with a long list of problems, asking a seller to repair every loose doorknob is a surefire deal-killer. Custom (not to mention common sense) dictates that buyers avoid asking for anything unreasonable. But what, exactly, is unreasonable? This will vary from place to place and market to market, and your real estate agent will be able to guide you toward what is and isn't a typical, reasonable request.

"Put yourself in the seller's shoes," says agent Shannon Jones. "If there are any health and safety concerns, most people would consider those repairs reasonable. But most sellers will say no if you come to them with a laundry list." In short, the right way to handle your inspection report is to avoid demanding the seller fix every little thing. Instead, take the time to sort out problems that are actually worth worrying about and negotiating over.

Deciding Which Repairs Matter

There are certain problems buyers typically ask sellers to handle. These include deferred maintenance, such as cleaning the pool or gutters, or having a neglected heating or air-conditioning system serviced. As always, local norms will guide what you ask for. "We have many septic systems and wells, and sellers typically pay for their septic systems to be pumped and inspected," says Marysville, Washington, agent Roy Van Winkle. "That's not written anywhere, but it's just expected."

The kinds of problems you encounter will depend on your region. Shifting foundations and termites are common in the South; basement leaks or insulation problems frequently occur up North. Your agent will be able to estimate what many common repairs will cost; in some cases, they may recommend calling in a contractor for an estimate. Once you see your repair estimate, you can decide what to ask the seller to fix and what you're prepared to repair (either with or without a repair allowance).

We suggest you exercise caution when deciding how to handle problems, such as leaks, electrical work, or pests, that require opening walls. It can often be difficult to tell how extensive such problems are from the outside, so when you open the wall, you may find a much larger problem than you bargained for. So, ask the seller to handle inside-the-wall repairs, if possible. Otherwise, you may negotiate a repair allowance of one amount, only to find once the drywall is in pieces that fixing the problem will cost five times more than you expected.

If you're thinking of taking on a major repair, we encourage you to factor in your short- and long-term plans. If you're staying only a few years, extensive repairs may not be worth the hassle. On the other hand, if this is the home you intend to live in for many years, it can be exciting to take the reins on an upgrade that will last a lifetime.

Understanding What You're Getting: the Unexpected Extras

Make sure you understand everything that you're getting with a property. While most single-family homes are relatively straightforward, there are some things to consider. For instance, out west, things like solar and wind power are becoming increasingly popular. But, if the solar panels on a home were purchased with a loan or simply leased instead of purchased outright, a buyer may have to take on that loan or renegotiate that lease. Similarly, if someone has agreed to allow a wind farm or power company to lease out a part of a property to place a windmill, the buyer may inherit or have to renegotiate those terms. (And, potentially, get paid an agreed-upon amount of money in return.)

Or, if you end up purchasing a house on a larger plot of land, or rural property, there are other things like mineral rights to consider. Mineral rights are the rights that apply to what's in the ground—oil, natural gas, and even coal. Most mineral rights aren't conveyed with the land purchase. Which means that, for instance, if someone comes and asks to drill for oil on your land, while you may get paid for allowing them to use your property, you don't have any claim to whatever they find. However, in some instances these rights are conveyed, and you may have a legal right to what's found on your land. All of this can be discussed more thoroughly with your agent.

Reaching Final Agreement

Once you've decided what you need to have fixed in order to make the purchase, your agent will convey your requests to the seller. Remember that your options include asking the seller to fix something or asking for a fixed sum so you can make the repairs yourself. The compensation can either be a reduction in the sales price or a cash repair allowance. And, if there isn't much wrong with the home, the simplest option is to move forward with the original contract without asking the seller to fix anything.

Once you get to the point of negotiating repairs, things can get a little tense. You're so close to having a deal but you're worried things might fall apart in negotiation. Still, all the emotions and excitement you and the seller feel can needlessly blow relatively minor issues—such as who will pay for the new $500 water heater in your $300,000 home—out of proportion. This is dangerous because the seller could reject your counter and kill the deal if it starts to seem like it will be easier to find another buyer than to come to an agreement. Good negotiating, then, means having a clear understanding of where you're willing to give as well as what matters most and communicating those priorities clearly to the seller. If negotiations prove difficult, you could decide you love the home enough to buy it, flaws and all. Should things come to an impasse, the inspection contingency will let you walk away.

However, there's a good chance you and the seller eventually will reach an agreement. At that point, you'll have a finalized contract and a homeowner's insurance policy (or at least you'll be well on your way to getting one). These two steps are probably the last big hurdles you'll have to face.

After the inspection and negotiation, you'll be at an exciting moment in your homeownership journey: when it becomes fairly certain that this home really will be yours. The last few steps between here and closing—which include a survey, title work, and appraisal—are handled primarily by your agent and lender and are explained in the next chapter.

Get a Homeowner's Insurance Policy

Having a homeowner's insurance policy is smart. It's also usually necessary—you can't get a mortgage without one. However, getting a policy on an older home can sometimes be complicated. Many insurance companies now require upgrades, renovations, and retrofitting, such as replacing outdated wiring, before they will issue a policy. So, get your inspection quickly, so you can find out what you need to update and can negotiate repairs with the seller, get them done, and have a policy in hand on closing day. "We have experienced varying degrees of challenges in terms of a home's insurability," notes agent Mike Duley, "but we almost always get it done."

To choose a policy, we recommend you start by calling a few companies referred by trusted and knowledgeable sources, including your real estate agent. Once they give you quotes, you can compare policies and premiums. Policies vary dramatically, so put in the time to choose the right one.

Shop Smart

When looking for insurance policies, we urge you, as always, to start with recommendations from people you know and your agent. However, insurance prices can vary a great deal from place to place, so take your time to shop around and find out which policy works best for you.

There are a number of great websites that can give you multiple insurance quotes. Places like Insurify and Keller Covered take the information about your home and deliver you a series of different quotes from top companies like Nationwide, Encompass, MetLife, and more. The more quotes you get, the more opportunities you have to find the perfect coverage at the perfect price. And don't be afraid to change your insurance or continue to shop around year after year—sometimes you can find better deals!

Choosing a Policy

A basic homeowner's insurance policy protects you in two ways. First, it insures against loss or damage to the property itself, such as a fire or hail damage. Second, it protects against liability in case someone sustains an injury while on your property, such as by slipping on ice in your driveway.

Generally speaking, homeowner's insurance policies fall into two major categories: **replacement cost** and **actual cash value**. Replacement cost insurance, while generally more expensive, offers more coverage. Generally, it will pay to rebuild your entire home as it was before an event, should your property be destroyed. Actual cash value coverage, while slightly less expensive, can end up offering less protection. This is chiefly because you are only awarded the current value of what was destroyed, which can be less than the current cost to replace it.

In both instances, your coverage will extend to other buildings on your property—not just your home. For example, if you have a shed or a detached garage, these will also be covered in the event that they are destroyed or damaged. Usually, these insurance policies will also help cover some of the contents of your home as well, up to a certain value. However, for high-value items, we recommend looking into separate, specialty coverage that will fully reimburse you for what you've lost. (We'll discuss this in detail shortly.)

Regardless of what type of insurance you go with, there are many ways you can add to or amend basic policies. Most insurance companies also offer varying **deductible rates**, which can impact your annual premium (i.e., the higher the deductible, the lower the premium). We believe the following questions will help you sort through your many options:

How Much Coverage Do I Need?

You don't have to buy insurance for the entire purchase price of your home. That price includes the cost of the land beneath it, which is virtually impossible to ruin, and which doesn't need to be insured. So, your $300,000 home may need only a $280,000 policy if the land beneath it is worth $20,000.

Should I Go for Replacement Cost or Actual Cash Value?

As we said, the biggest choice you'll make for your policy is going with replacement cost or actual cash value. If you go with actual cash value, that value is the price of the home: if the home you insure today for $250,000 burns down ten years from now, you will be given $250,000 with which to replace it. Unfortunately for actual cash value policyholders, increasing construction costs means that $250,000 will buy less and less house as the years go by. That's why most buyers choose a replacement-cost policy, which is a little more expensive, but will pay for rebuilding your home, no matter the cost.

What Are the Named and Unnamed Perils?

Home damage can come in many forms—from the usual suspects, such as fires or break-ins, to the bizarre... meteorites, runaway trucks, or even escaped circus animals. The best policy is **all-peril**: it covers damage from anything not specifically excluded in the policy language. This insurance is a little more expensive, but it protects against surprises. A named-peril policy covers only damage that is specifically listed in the policy. If you accept the risk of a named-peril policy, be sure you understand exactly what the policy does and doesn't cover.

Do I Need Personal Property Insurance?

If your home was damaged or destroyed, it's unlikely that your possessions would survive unscathed. And that personal property represents a lot of money. Once you add up what it would cost to replace all your possessions, from your socks to your dishes to your furniture, it's obvious why so many buyers add **personal property insurance** to their policies. If you own extremely valuable or one-of-a-kind possessions, such as fine jewelry or art, you can purchase additional coverage on top of the standard amount. Be sure you check whether a personal property policy will cover your possessions no matter where the loss or damage occurs. If your laptop is stolen when you're on vacation, for example, this kind of policy can be beneficial.

What Are My Additional Living Expenses?

You may need to consider adding these to your policy if you need to cover additional costs—if, for example, you're stuck in a hotel for a month while damage to your home is repaired.

A Quick Reminder: Warranties

Warranties and insurance seem similar, but they cover different things. Namely, warranties cover repairs or replacement of appliances and major systems within your home. For instance, if your cooling unit breaks down—that's more of a warranty problem than an insurance one. Insurance, on the other hand, would cover replacing part of your house if the unit broke and sparked a fire that damaged the house. Combined, warranties and insurance create a blanket of protection for your home.

Specialized Insurance

Your standard policy most likely won't cover damage from geographically predictable perils, such as hurricanes in Florida. If you live on a coast, you may want to consider purchasing extra protection. In fact, it may be required. The same is true for earthquakes in California. If you live near a fault line, you'll be on shaky ground without earthquake insurance, even though the damage is not your fault. Specialized insurance is also available for some other types of liability.

Flood Insurance

While most basic insurance covers some damage, most flood damage is not covered in an average policy. And, if you're a buyer purchasing a home in a flood-prone area, some states often require buyers to purchase flood insurance as a condition for approving the mortgage. Luckily, flood insurance is relatively easy to get. In the United States, you can get basic flood insurance through the National Flood Insurance Program (*www. floodsmart.gov*), as well as some private insurers. For Canadian residents, the best place to check for flood insurance is through the Insurance Bureau of Canada (*www.ibc.ca/qc/*).

Earthquake Insurance

In places where earthquakes are common, earthquake insurance is often required. That way, should one hit and your property get damaged, you'll be protected and your home can be rebuilt. According to the US Geological Survey, the top two states for seismic activity in the United States are California and Alaska, but states including Tennessee, Oregon, and more have been known to have the occasional quake. Depending on what state you're in, there may be a local source through which you can be insured, like the California Earthquake Authority. Or, as always, there are private insurers who can provide you with coverage.

Proof and Prepayment

Once you choose a policy, your company will send proof of insurance to your lender that officially clears one of the hurdles on your road to closing. The insurance company will also make arrangements for you to prepay a year's worth of premiums as part of your closing costs. With that out of the way, you're on to the next exciting final step in the path to homeownership: closing.

Notes to Take Home

The property inspection (which we recommend you attend) should expose the hidden issues a home might have, so you know exactly what you are getting into before you sign closing papers.

- Your main concern is the possibility of structural damage. This can come from water damage, shifting ground, or poor construction when the house was built.

- Don't sweat the small stuff. It's the inspector's job to mark everything discovered, no matter how large or small. Things that are easily fixed can be overlooked.

- If you have a big problem show up in your inspection report, you should bring in a specialist. And if the worst-case scenario turns out to be true, you might want to walk away from the purchase.

A homeowner's insurance policy protects you in two ways:

- Against loss or damage to the property itself.

- Against liability in case someone sustains an injury while on your property.

MO ANDERSON'S FIRST HOME

Growing up the daughter of a tenant farmer in Enid, Oklahoma, I always dreamed of owning my own home. My husband and I were thirty years old with two small children and living in a rental house in nearby Ponca City when God finally answered our prayers. We had saved a small amount of money for a down payment and put together a wish list. Then, we learned that our neighbors who lived two doors down were planning to sell their house.

The house had everything we wanted: three bed-rooms, two baths, and a nice-sized backyard for the children. It also had two big selling points—a large main bedroom that had been added and a huge family room with a fireplace and hearth. That big room is what sold us! I could see our families gathering around that

---

* Photograph courtesy of the Anderson family.

big fireplace during holidays—our parents and siblings, nieces and nephews. All that, and it was in our price range—less than $20,000.

Excitedly, we approached our neighbors about buying their house. We purchased without the guidance of an agent, and our neighbors sold to us without an agent so they could save the cost of the commission. In retrospect, the transaction was not the easiest, but I still remember the thrill of finally having a home of our own and no longer being a renter.

Soon after we moved in, it started raining following a long drought. The house leaked like a sieve! We had to put buckets everywhere to keep from getting soaked. What a difficult turn of events for a young couple with two children and very limited finances. We had to use the money we had set aside to buy furniture to fix the roof instead. So, while our neighbors had saved a little money, we learned an important, costly lesson. From then on, we always used an agent.

Although we got off to a rocky start, I have wonderful memories of our first home: raising our children, visiting with our great neighbors, watching our kids run in and out of the house and play in our backyard. All those dreams I had of sharing Thanksgiving and Christmas gatherings with the people we loved most sitting around that wonderful fireplace in our family room came true. It was even better than I had imagined.

We sold that house twelve years later for about $28,000 and put our equity into a brand-new home with 2,800 square feet. It felt like we had moved into a mansion. We still own that second home and stay there whenever we go back to Ponca City.

Our first little house taught us a lot. I learned that owning a home is a big responsibility. You have to keep up your house and lawn even when you don't have much money because that's part of being a good neighbor.

One of the biggest lessons I learned was not to let fear influence your decisions. When we bought our first home, we also had the option of buying a new one for just over $5,000 more. As a financially strapped young family, that amount scared us to death—even though we qualified to purchase it. That house sold for $50,000—around the same time we sold ours. The owners doubled their investment!

Most of all, I learned the joys of homeownership. As a tenant farmer's daughter, I probably appreciated it more than most people. After all this time and all the houses we have owned, I still do.

Mo Anderson is vice chairman of the board of Keller Williams Realty.

CHAPTER 8

CLOSE

The week before closing on her house was an emotional one for Becky Pastner of Austin, Texas. She was crazy about the adorable bungalow she had found and thrilled at the prospect of becoming a homeowner at the age of twenty-six. Still, she found herself in tears the night before closing. "I was happy to be buying a home," Becky recalls, "but I was just so full of emotions."

She was tense and jittery the next morning, as she and her husband drove through a downpour to their lender's office. They were so nervous they got lost on the way. Everything changed, however, the moment they sat down at the closing table. "As soon as we got inside, I knew everything was going to be okay," says Becky. The storm even blew over while they were signing their paperwork. When Becky stepped outside, the bright sunshine seemed to perfectly reflect her elation at finally owning her own home.

As your closing day approaches, you might be feeling as anxious as a long-tailed cat in a room full of rocking chairs. That's understandable and normal—you're making a large decision that will quite literally change almost every aspect of your life. But take a breath, and remind yourself that you're in the homestretch. And soon, you'll be waking up in your very own home.

Even though the final stage of the home-buying process can let loose a lot of feelings, it is really all about checking off boxes. In your closing stage, your agent and lender will be focused on verifying that everything is as it should be: making sure your finances are in order, finishing any paperwork, and doing some final checks on the house. They will also confirm the home's value and legal status with the lender, which includes a survey, appraisal, title search, and a final check of your credit and finances. Your agent will keep you posted on how each is progressing, but unlike the previous hands-on stages of your home-buying adventure, your work is pretty much done. At this point, you don't have much to worry about other than keeping your finances tight and your credit clean. You'll also need to confirm with your agent that you'll have all the necessary documents and funds you'll need so you can move smoothly into your closing day—and into your new life as a homeowner.

Preclosing Verifications

As closing day approaches, your lender and agent will do most of the work. However, to help the process go smoothly, you should make sure you do the following:

1. Stay in control of your finances.

2. Return all phone calls and paperwork promptly.

3. Communicate with your agent at least once a week.

4. Several days before closing, confirm with your agent that all your documentation is in place and in order.

5. Obtain certified funds for closing.

6. Conduct a final walk-through.

Final Verifications for the Lender

Just as you confirmed the value of your future home through a property inspection, lending institutions also take certain steps before finalizing a mortgage to make sure they are backing a sound investment. These include the following:

- An appraisal to confirm the value of the property
- A survey to confirm the legal boundaries and entitlements of the property
- A title search to verify the ownership of the property
- Title insurance to protect against mistakes in the title search

Chances are good that these final steps—which, incidentally, you will pay for as part of your closing costs—will go smoothly. The whole point of these preclosing verifications is to look for problems that occasionally arise. If you run into a patch of trouble, think of it this way: you'll feel lucky if a title search or survey reveals a property's questionable ownership or boundaries *before* closing, rather than after the house is already yours.

Appraisal

Imagine a buyer takes out a $300,000 loan on a home and promptly defaults. If your lending institution can't resell that house for at least $300,000, it loses money. To protect against that possibility, your lender will require an independent appraisal of your home's value before finalizing your mortgage. An appraiser does exactly what you and your agent did when you were deciding how much to offer for your home: they compare the property you're buying to others in the area in terms of size, condition, location, and amenities. In most cases, appraisers generate a reasonable fair market value, one which falls in the same range that buyers discover.

Every once in a while, though, appraisers think homes are worth less than what the buyer and seller have agreed to. This can happen for several reasons. For instance, perhaps the seller made an addition without getting necessary permits, so appraisers can't legally count that new square footage in the home's value. Or buyers in fast-moving markets offer more than the asking price to make sure their offer is accepted.

Your lender won't write a loan for more than a home's appraised value, so if your appraisal comes in low, you'll have to figure out a way to cover the gap. For example, let's say you're under contract for a $350,000 home, and you planned to put $70,000 down and borrow $280,000. If the property appraises for $340,000 and the lender will only lend you $270,000, you will have to come up with the shortfall and pay an additional $10,000 down to close. In situations like these, sometimes the seller lowers the price, sometimes the buyer pays the extra cash, or sometimes the buyer and seller split the difference. You can also dispute the appraisal and ask the lender to order a new appraisal. (This is definitely worth a shot if you think the appraiser misjudged a fast-moving market.)

If all else fails, and either you are unable to cover the difference of value or you don't trust the appraised value, you aren't trapped. You can exercise the financing contingency in your contract and walk away. Note that conditions often have expiration dates in Canada. Be sure to find out what you need to know about your home, such as the appraisal, before any financing condition expires.

Survey

When neighborhoods are new, it's obvious where one yard ends and another begins. But as the years pass and people build fences, sheds, and additions, the boundaries can blur. When property lines become muddled, a survey of the properties comes in handy. It provides a bird's-eye view of the property lines to make sure your new home and any structures on the property don't touch or cross any boundaries. It also confirms the location of easements, which are areas where property owners aren't supposed to build. The most common easements are for utilities and allow government entities permanent access to power and sewer lines. That access includes the right to tear down anything within the easement that would keep these entities from working. It may seem easy to avoid building a new dining room within an easement, but every agent has a story about the longtime homeowner who had a pool, addition, or detached garage built and meant to check for easements but forgot.

Surveys can also protect you from downright fraudulent sales. While not common, there have been instances of homeowners who have assumed they were buying one particular parcel of land, or a specific property, only to find out they were mistaken. In fact, they've only bought a portion of what they thought. But a survey, when done correctly, will show you the entire scope of what you do—or don't—own.

If a seller has a recent survey, lenders will usually accept it. However, if the survey is more than a few years old, lenders usually require a new one. Typically, the lender commissions the survey, and you the buyer pay for it as part of your closing costs. You keep the survey at closing, so make sure you save it in a safe place, whether that's in a physical location like a personal safe, or in a folder on your computer dedicated to your homeownership documents. That way, when you decide to build an addition, you'll know where *not* to put the new dining room!

Title

It's surprising enough that homeowners sometimes forget the precise locations of their property lines. More shocking is the kind of confusion that can arise over who has legal ownership, or title, to a piece of property. Factors such as divorce, death, and debts can create legal conundrums over who has the legal right to call a house "my home."

Agents and loan officers have seen just about everything. Austin, Texas, loan officer Barbara Frierson recalls a closing that got held up when the home being sold belonged to a homeowner who died without a will, forcing the title company to track down every potential heir coming to approve the deal before it could close. "I probably have enough stories to write a book! There was one case where the people selling the house were not the owners," she says. "If it hadn't been for the title company, no one would have known."

These sorts of problems are why lenders require a title search and **title insurance** before closing. Getting a title search is like getting screened for rare diseases with your doctor at your annual checkup: there probably won't be a problem, but if there is, you need to know about it right away. A title company (or, in Canada, a real estate lawyer) protects your deal by researching the title for liens, **encumbrances** (claims against property), and other potential problems. In addition to disputed ownership, title searches protect you from unpaid liens, which are claims against the seller's debts. For example, you don't want to buy a home from someone in a dispute with the IRS (or its Canadian equivalent, the Canada Revenue Agency) over unpaid taxes—if the IRS goes after the property, you could get caught in the middle.

Even with all that searching, title companies sometimes miss things. That's why your lender will also require you to buy title insurance that covers your costs if, for example, a missing heir does show up a few years down the road. Title insurance also covers mistakes in survey interpretation.

Closing Preparations for You:
Keep Yourself Mortgage Worthy

You may be a minor player in the appraisal and title work, but when it comes to finalizing your mortgage, you're still the star. Your lender will check your finances just before approving your loan for the final time at closing. They are looking to make sure you're in the same good financial shape you were in when the lender preapproved you a month or two ago. Your job is to remain that creditworthy person: keep your discretionary spending to a minimum, don't buy anything on credit, and—whatever you do—don't spend your cash reserves.

"When it comes to keeping financial profiles in good shape until closing, we have a list of do's and don'ts," says Cleveland, Ohio, agent Ed Huck. "For example, don't open any other lines of credit for anything—car, furniture, anything. Document all deposits into your accounts. Do not make any large deposits or withdrawals without explanations and a paper trail."

Unfortunately, every agent has a story about buyers who didn't realize they needed to keep their financial profiles spotless right up until closing. In their excitement to settle into their beautiful new homes, some buyers jump the gun and buy furniture and appliances. Then, when the lender pulls their credit, they find that their scores have dropped, sometimes so much that they no longer qualify for a loan.

"I worked with a couple who bought a truckload of furniture on credit just before closing," says agent Don Beach in Tulsa, Oklahoma. "They had marginal credit to begin with, and those purchases pushed them out of the acceptable range. We found out the night before closing."

Fortunately, Don was able to strike an agreement with the furniture company to "return" the furniture until the deal was closed. The move restored the couple's credit, so despite a few frantic, stressful hours, they ended up with both the home *and* the furniture.

Buying furniture isn't the only way buyers jeopardize their transactions. Some carelessly spend their down payment or the money they had put away for closing costs. This can lead to some frantic maneuvers to find cash at the last minute. "We call it the Tesla clause," Austin, Texas, mortgage lender branch manager Zander Blunt says. "We have some people buy cars a few days before closing. I've seen everything from BMWs and Teslas to boats. We had a client who bought a car, and he had to take it back the next day in order to close. He closed on his house a day later, and *then* went back to buy the car again—and this time they charged him a higher price."

Spare yourself the tension: go into a financial deep freeze as soon as you start home shopping. Tighten your belt, pinch your pennies, let your clothing get as threadbare as these clichés. Don't make any major purchases and keep your minor spending in check. After all, you'll be able to make extra spending decisions once you officially own your home.

Surviving Setbacks

No matter how careful you and your team have been, deals do fall apart at the last minute, even at the closing table. So, don't be shocked if a glitch occurs and has to be ironed out at the last minute. This happens all the time. Murphy's Law—a famous adage that states that whatever can go wrong, will go wrong—comes into play more often than not when it's closing time. Just be patient and things should fall into place. After all, there are so many documents and people involved in a closing—so many moving parts—that something, somewhere can stop the whole machine temporarily.

If something does stall the closing, that's all it usually is: stalled. Things should be rectified in a few hours or days. However, sometimes deals really do fall apart in a serious way. This can happen for any number of reasons, and we know it can feel devastating. It can seem like so much work, so much effort, so much preparation has been for nothing.

But it's not all for nothing. Having a deal fall apart is a setback and a disappointment, to be sure. But even if you have to search for a different home, much of the work is already behind you: you've received a solid market education. You know what you're looking for. You know a good inspector, a good lender, and a good agent. So, you've got a whole team already in place the moment you're ready to dust yourself off and get back on track.

Countdown to Closing

Once you and the home have checked out, you'll receive your final loan commitment. Only then will the closing company schedule a time and place for the closing. (In Canada, this should be discussed with your lawyer.) As the big day approaches, confirm with the appropriate parties that you have everything you need in order to close and transition smoothly into your new home. This will include the following:

1. Settlement statement
2. Certified funds
3. Evidence of insurance

Settlement Statement

Also known as a closing statement, the settlement statement is a final, official rendering of the terms of your loan and your exact closing costs. It's sometimes called a "HUD" or "HUD-1" statement, which was the name on the form until 2015, when it was changed to the "Closing Disclosure" form. Rolls off the tongue, right? Most larger loans of any type require lenders to create a settlement statement for your review that explicitly states what all of the fees and expectations are. By law, your lender must provide it at least a day before closing. If you request it sooner, however, you'll have more time to compare it with your good-faith estimate.

In essence, the settlement statement is a line-by-line breakdown of the costs associated with purchasing your home. It lists out the terms and conditions of the settlement you and all other parties have agreed to. While you may have serious document fatigue and be ready to get started on moving into your new home, it's important to take the time to carefully review your settlement statement with your agent. It's your final chance you have to make sure that everything you're about to sign is in line with what you've discussed or been told previously.

For instance, maybe you look over the document and find that your interest rate or any fees are higher than what you were promised—in which case we advise you to call your agent immediately. This is also a good time to have your agent explain any fees you still don't understand, so you can feel as confident as possible on closing day.

Certified Funds

When you're buying a property, you can't just whip out your checkbook at the closing table. You will need to pay your down payment and closing costs with certified funds from a financial institution. Certified funds are important in larger transactions like real estate for one simple reason: unlike a regular check, certified funds can't bounce. They're *certified*, which means there's a guarantee they are there. This prevents any faulty funds from creating a snarl in the transaction.

Once you have a settlement statement, you can go to your bank and get the precise amount of funds you'll need in the form of a cashier's check or by having your bank wire that amount to your closing escrow account.

Evidence of Insurance

The final part of getting things squared and finalized with your lender is presenting proof of homeowner's insurance (which also shows that the house is, in fact, insurable). This comes in the form of an evidence of insurance letter from whatever company your new home is now insured through. *Don't forget, part of that evidence is prepaying a year's worth of insurance premiums.*

Final Walk-Through

The day before closing, you'll get the opportunity to stroll through the home that will soon be yours. Take a deep breath. Feel proud. And then, look carefully around. The final walk-through provides your last chance to make sure the home is clean and all requested repairs have been made. If by some chance something is left undone, let your agent know immediately so she can negotiate with the seller's agent—for example, by asking for them to leave some money in the escrow account to cover the repair cost. We recommend a final walk-through as a great way to avoid problems and relieve worry, but please note that it is not always a part of the typical closing process. Your agent will have to request this from the seller and possibly make it a condition in your contract, but that doesn't mean it's difficult. You just have to ask.

Questions for the Final Walk-Through

1. Is the house clean, and are the seller's possessions removed? If *not*, when will they be?

2. Are all the required repairs made? Did you request and receive documentation of when repairs were made and who made them?

3. Do you have all the items needed for the house (codes, openers, manuals, and warranty information, among others)? If *not*, when will you receive them?

Even if the home is sparkling and the repairs look impeccable, make sure you get documentation stating that the repairs have been completed, as well as who did the actual work. First of all, your insurance or home warranty company may require documentation of the repairs at some point. In addition, even the best contractors occasionally slip up: if that just-repaired pipe springs another leak two weeks after closing, you need to know who can fix the problem. This is also the ideal time to get all the detailed information you'll need as the home's new owner, such as security access codes, garage door openers, and appliance manuals.

Closing Day

Closing day is a life-changing event: you walk in a renter and walk out a homeowner. Whatever you feel the morning you wake up to close, there's one thing you can count on—you're prepared. "By the time I got to closing, I had learned so much about escrow, points, real estate taxes, and everything else that it didn't matter to me that the closing itself was pretty much a mystery," remembers Oklahoma buyer Tonja Pitzer. "I had someone I trusted guiding me through, saying, 'Sign here; sign here.'"

On closing day, you can expect to sit at a table with a bunch of pens and sign your name so many times you start to feel like Captain Kirk at a *Star Trek* convention. Other than that, the procedures vary dramatically from province to province, state to state, and even city to city. The settlement agent who runs the show may be an attorney, a representative of a title company, or someone else entirely. You may be sitting across the table from the seller, or you may be all the way across town. Your agent or a member of the agent's team may attend to explain any last-minute questions. There are a myriad of variables depending on where you live. In any case, the settlement agent can usually explain everything as you sign documents. During this process you will:

1. Finalize your mortgage
2. Pay the seller
3. Pay your closing costs
4. Transfer the title from the seller to you
5. Make arrangements to legally record the transaction as public record

You might get the keys immediately, or the key handover might take place only after the funds clear and the transaction is legally recorded. And it's possible there may be a hiccup or two—for example, one woman's husband forgot to sign his middle name on one of the forms, and the lender had to correct the error before the couple could get their home keys. But as long as you have clear expectations and follow directions, closing should be a momentous conclusion to your home-searching process and commencement of your home-owning experience.

Closing Night

And then, suddenly, it's all over. You're no longer a renter. You're no longer a home seeker or a home buyer. You're a *homeowner*! That means you're building up equity, enjoying tax benefits, and reveling in the freedom to paint your dining room any color you please.

Homeownership is a source of pride, contentment, and security. You have an entire place to start this exciting new phase of life in and make your own. However, homeownership does come with responsibilities. Some of them are fun responsibilities, such as sprucing up the yard. Others, we must admit, can be a hassle, such as dealing with the first maintenance emergency. Fortunately, the relationship you've built with your agent doesn't end the day the deal closes. Full-service agents pride themselves on being there to answer your questions, look out for your needs, and provide service for a lifetime. Chapter 10 offers some ideas on how to take advantage of this opportunity.

Notes to Take Home

- Your preclosing responsibilities include:

    - Staying in control of your finances.

    - Returning all phone calls and paperwork promptly.

    - Communicating with your agent at least once a week.

    - Several days before closing, confirming with your agent that all documentation is in place and in order.

    - Obtaining certified funds for closing.

    - Conducting a final walk-through.

- Be sure you know the time and place for closing.

- Confirm with your agent that you have the following lined up and ready to go:

    - Settlement statement—the final, official rendering of the terms of your loan and your exact closing costs.

    - Certified funds—the exact dollar amount you'll need for closing in the form of a cashier's check or other guaranteed funds.

    - Evidence of insurance—proof that you have secured your homeowner's insurance, which comes in the form of an "evidence of insurance" letter from your company.

- Your agent is there to help you navigate the ups and downs of homeownership, even after the initial purchase is over.

SHARON GIBBONS' FIRST HOME

"You can't afford it." That's the first thing my mother said when my husband and I told her about the plans to buy our first home. My dad, on the other hand, caved in as soon as he saw the size of the big garage. He promptly brought his boat over.

I can't say I blame my mother for being nervous. We were very young and newly married—both of us full-time students and part-time employees. But my husband and I thought buying a house made perfect sense. First, it was located in the area where we had grown up, Galena Park, Texas, where we knew everyone. Second, the asking price of $18,000 sure seemed like a sweet deal. We would be making payments on a home of our own for a little more than our monthly rent.

I smile now reflecting on that twenty-one-year-old

---

* Photograph courtesy of the Gibbons family.

moving into her first home. She instantly felt so mature and domesticated. All the women in both of our families had gardens and did their own pickling and canning. So, I eagerly followed in their footsteps, using the home's ancient kitchen stove that came with the house to make fig preserves and jams. I can still remember the preserves bubbling in a cooking pot and the heat from that stove during those long Texas summers. My husband, meanwhile, fixed my father's boat, moved it out, and put that two-car garage to good use on various other projects. He even overhauled one of the engines of our cars.

We had so much fun in that house. It had beautiful trees in the backyard and was close to everything, including our families and childhood friends. Looking back, it seems we had parties and get-togethers almost every week. When we sold it three years later to build a home and start our family, we even made a small profit!

Homeownership has always been important in my family. Growing up during the Depression, my parents firmly believed that as long as you owned your own property—with room enough for a small garden—you'd be secure.

When my daughter was twenty, I relived the thrill of first-time homeownership by helping her buy her first home. She found a nice little place, and we helped her finance it for fifteen years, which means that by the time she's thirty-five, she'll own it free and clear.

I loved being able to help my child live the American Dream. I also have the satisfaction of knowing that no matter what might happen, she will always have a home. In a sense, I'm passing the advice my parents gave to me—the importance of homeownership—to the next generation.

Sharon Gibbons is treasurer of KW Cares and one of the first employees at Keller Williams Realty.

CHAPTER 9

MOVE IN AND PROTECT YOUR INVESTMENT

You don't need a book to tell you that the day you finally move into your own home will be one of the most exciting of your life. It's a major accomplishment—a huge milestone in adulthood and an incredible financial investment—something to celebrate. In fact, as long as you live in your home, you'll still feel a surge of pride every time someone admires your garden or compliments your framed concert posters.

Pride of ownership is only one of the ways your life will change as a homeowner. You can build equity, start a family, plant a garden—the sky's the limit. Your new home comes with new privileges but also with new responsibilities. For starters, the whole process of moving includes a lot of parts, utilities, movers, mail keys, and much more. Other responsibilities will develop over time, like home maintenance. It may all seem confusing at first, but don't worry—like every stage you went through in the home-buying process, you'll learn to make the most of your home one step at a time. And you'll always have your agent just a call away, ready to offer advice and opinions long after you've settled into your home.

Settling In

Although you may feel like you've crossed the finish line when the ink has dried on your paperwork, the exercise is not quite over. There's still a little left to do as you literally move into your first home. So, yes, hurry over the moment you get your hand on the keys—bask in the fact that this house is *yours*—and then roll up your sleeves to finish the journey. Here are some of the last steps you'll need to take to ensure that your move-in day is just as perfect as you imagined.

1. Transfer Utilities

Maybe you're thinking about celebrating your new home with a candlelit dinner, on account of how *fancy* you are. However, candles will be your only option if you forgot to transfer the utilities into your name and have no electricity. Might be nice for one night, but trust us, this is a modern convenience you don't want to be without for long.

A couple of weeks before closing, you should contact all the appropriate utility and service providers (gas, electricity, water, garbage, telephone, cable, among others) to arrange for transfer of services on your tentative closing date. Set a reminder to transfer utilities as soon as possible, so you avoid having your services interrupted. Typically, most service companies will allow for an overlap of accounts at two addresses, so service remains intact during the move-in-move-out process.

Typical Utilities to Check On

There is a myriad of different things that need to get handled when it's time to move, and most of those things are utilities. Before your move-in date, you'll want to review this list and make sure you've scheduled your utilities to transfer. (Or, if the utility service providers are different, that you've ended one service and begun another.)

- Electric
- Water
- Gas
- Internet
- Cable
- Trash
- Recycling

2. Schedule Movers

If you want a move with minimal hassle, many agents recommend hiring movers. However, the decision whether or not to use them is a personal one. It often depends on how much cash is on hand after a home purchase and how much stuff you have to move. If you plan to use movers, schedule them as soon as possible (a month out would be about right). You should hire a moving company the same way you hire any other professional: collect referrals from satisfied customers. After all, some of the most irreplaceable things in our homes (like your collection of vintage vinyl), have virtually no financial value, but that doesn't mean they shouldn't be handled with care.

3. Take Care of Your Mail

If you're moving into a home with a shiny mailbox on your lawn or nestled against your walls, then the only thing you'll need to worry about is changing your address with the United States Postal Service. (This can be done easily online at *moversguide.usps.com* in the United States or via the Canada Post website at *canadapost.ca* for Canadians.)

However, if you live in a neighborhood with community mailboxes, things can be a bit more involved. Instead of simply taking the old mail key, you'll have to go to your local post office and get assigned a new box. This requires two things: ID and proof of homeownership. Once you present the two, you'll be assigned a new box and then called back in a few days to pick up your new keys and any mail you may have missed.

Pack Smart

Unpacking and getting settled can take a couple of days, especially if you're doing it all yourselves. When you're packing and preparing to move into your new house, remember to set a few necessities aside, so you'll have what you need before you finish unpacking. That means gathering up at least a week's worth of clothes, some basic kitchen staples, first aid, and plastic silverware and plates. It's important to make sure you've got the basics you'll need to get through the day—even if you haven't found that box of shoes yet!

Good Home Habits

So, you've finally moved in! Maybe you've even started transforming your new home: buying rugs, arranging furniture, and painting. Part of the joy of owning your home is being able to make it look how you want it to look. But it's also important to keep your house in top condition. It's true that remembering to clean the gutters or change the air filters isn't nearly as exciting as putting a dashing new coat of paint on the living room walls. However, attention to your home maintenance needs—even if you never pick up a screwdriver yourself—is essential to protecting the long-term value of your investment.

Home maintenance falls into two main categories, which we'll call "keeping it clean" and "keeping an eye on it." Keeping things clean includes the basic things we do every day: vacuuming, wiping off counters, and keeping things tidy. But there are major systems in your home that need to be cleaned and maintained, much like the oil needs to be changed in your car. Some things you can easily do yourself, like cleaning the gutters. However, some systems do best with regular attention by a professional—particularly the heating and air-conditioning systems.

After you're settled into your home and the boxes are unpacked, we encourage you to review the maintenance needs of your home's systems and come up with a plan for regular service. Agent Dakoda Reece of Geneva, Illinois, advises, "Create a schedule and mark your calendar for when to do things like change the filters, clean out the gutters, and so on and so forth. This will keep everything top of mind." This kind of maintenance not only helps prevent major disasters; it also ensures your systems will be covered by your home warranty when they do break.

In addition, smart homeowners watch for new stains, cracks, peeling, or other warning signs that damage may be imminent—things you need to keep an eye on. For example, deteriorating caulk around windows doesn't seem like a big deal, but it's one of the major culprits in mold growth. Noticing these problems sooner rather than later can keep a small problem from developing into a big one or causing a second problem. Fixing a leak in the plumbing, for example, is nothing compared to fixing the leak *plus* a year or two of moisture damage to your flooring or walls. If you need a more dramatic example, imagine the difference a fresh pair of batteries makes in the smoke detector!

Good Home Habits

Keeping It Clean

Perform routine maintenance on your home's systems, depending on their age and style.

In general, your list should include the following:

1. Clean your gutters once a year.
2. Change your air filters every two to three months or when they appear dirty.
3. Have your heating and air-conditioning professionally serviced once a year.
4. Change the batteries in your smoke detectors once a year.
5. Read your appliance manuals for recommended upkeep, such as changing your refrigerator's water filter.

Keeping an Eye on It

Watch for signs of leaks, damage, and wear. Fixing small problems early can save you big money later.

Items to be aware of include:

1. Cracks in the ceiling or walls could indicate foundation problems.
2. Water stains indicate leaks, which need to be fixed as soon as possible.
3. Eroding caulk around doors and windows can let in moisture that causes dangerous mold growth inside your walls.
4. Buckling or faded shingles indicate your roof is nearing the end of its life.
5. Tree branches scraping your roof can damage shingles and allow pests access to your home.
6. Be on the lookout for signs of pests common to your area.

Figure 9.1

Maintaining your home is also a smart financial decision. For one thing, it helps you create the potential for future investment through renting or selling. Maybe you'll decide you want to get a slightly larger home down the line, but instead of selling your first home, you decide to turn it into a rental property. That way, renters could help you pay off the original mortgage on your first home (if you haven't already), and you can pocket some extra income.

Second, maintaining your home ensures that you're able to later sell your home and put that money down toward a new one. But, if you want to make a fair bit of change, you'll need to make sure your home reflects the best that's on that future market. It's important to remember that your new home is an investment toward your future real estate holdings. It's a great way to leverage equity and grow your portfolio. And all it requires is a little attentiveness, knowledge, and money. You can stay on top of these requirements by utilizing your home warranty and by keeping maintenance cash reserves.

Getting the Most Out of Home Warranties

Home warranties are increasingly popular deal sweeteners for many buyers. Even if you didn't get one from the seller, you can buy one for yourself. (But remember—home warranties aren't the same as insurance and usually only cover your home for a period of time.) If the seller chose the policy, you can usually make changes to what is covered within the first month of owning your home. Be sure to read the fine print—most policies exclude certain appliances or systems, so you may be in for a surprise if you find out the refrigerator is not covered only *after* it goes warm. And we suggest you make any changes as soon as possible. Warranty companies don't want you to wait for the water heater to break and then add it to your coverage if it wasn't originally covered, so they usually require a technician to certify its condition (at your cost) if you want to add coverage further down the road.

To get the most out of your home warranty, make sure you understand what might cause the warranty company to deny coverage. For instance, some companies use poor maintenance as a reason for denial. Others may not cover repairs that were reviewed by someone the warranty provider didn't send. For example, if your air conditioner dies and you ask Joe, the HVAC technician next door, to look at it before you call the warranty company, the latter might deny coverage. So, make sure you're smart, and go through the proper steps and channels your warranty provider requires.

Warranties cost several hundred dollars annually. So, many buyers, especially ones with new homes, decide their money would be better spent making repairs themselves. But those who have had warranties cover a several-thousand-dollar job often swear by their long-term value.

Budget for Maintenance

Whether or not you have a warranty, you should definitely have a maintenance budget. Depending on the size and age of your home, you can expect to spend several hundred to several thousand dollars on maintenance each year. Budgeting for these costs will ease the crunch in an emergency, and it will also help you stay on top of seemingly minor problems that can grow worse over time. If you don't end up spending all your reserves, you can always use the cash for fun home-improvement projects, such as retiling the bathroom or landscaping the backyard.

In the end, the responsibilities that come with owning a home are dwarfed by the joys and privileges of homeownership. The last step in your home-buying process should be obvious—it's time to celebrate!

Celebrate!

You've finally made it to the end of your home-buying journey and to the beginning of life as a homeowner. Different people celebrate this accomplishment in different ways. Some people throw a big party to meet all their new neighbors. Some people go on a painting blitz or plant a half-dozen new trees. Some people just want to sit on the couch, gaze admiringly at the walls and ceiling, and feel all tingly. And, for many owners, one of the most fulfilling ways to celebrate the opportunity and privilege of owning their own homes is by getting involved in their neighborhoods.

After all, it's natural that when you're putting down roots, you start thinking about ways to improve the soil. As people settle into their new neighborhoods, many homeowners find their new commitment makes them think about and want to get involved in their communities in new ways—from cleaning up parks and buying cookies from the Girl Scouts, to serving as precinct captains for their political party and volunteering in their churches, synagogues, and mosques, to joining Facebook groups made up of all their neighbors. Whatever form it takes, many homeowners find that the connection between owning a home they care about and caring about the people in their neighborhood brings the benefits of ownership to a whole new level.

We wish you the best in making the most of your new home and filling it with good moments and lasting memories. This is something Datri Gasser thinks about as she slowly updates the gracious 1920s home she bought in Seattle, Washington. The previous owner, an elderly woman named Marjorie, lived there for fifty-three years. In that time Marjorie had taken exquisite care of her home, filling it with the relics from half a century of living. Datri has no plans to stay put nearly as long, but as she looks toward the years ahead, she still feels a sense of permanence. "We have a deep respect for our house because Marjorie took such good care of it," she says. "We want to do the same, to take care of it and appreciate it, and then pass it on to someone else."

Although Datri and her husband have lived in their home for several years, the excitement of owning it never seems to wear off. "We felt so lucky when we bought our home," says Datri. "We still feel lucky every day."

Notes to Take Home

- Make sure you have movers scheduled, utilities transferred, and all of your ducks in a row for a smooth move-in.

- Perform routine maintenance on your home's systems, depending on their age and condition.

- Watch for signs of leaks, damage, and wear. Fixing small problems early will save you big money later.

- Take pride in homeownership, enjoy its benefits, and visit *YourFirstHomeBook.com* for worksheets and other helpful resources.

TERESA METCALF'S FIRST HOME

My family moved around when I was a child, so it wasn't until I was in late elementary school that my parents purchased their first home in Dunn, North Carolina. When I think about that house, it's not the ranch-style home itself that comes to mind but the activities that surrounded it, like how we played with our two poodles in the fenced-in backyard.

When my husband and I first got married, we lived in a great little two-bedroom duplex. My stepson was about ten at the time, so it was the perfect fit—each of us had a bedroom. However, things changed once we had a baby on the way. Our cute little duplex didn't have enough space for another child. It was time for us to buy our first home.

Looking back on it, I know things turned out exactly

Photograph courtesy of Ashley Reis.

as they were meant to be. At the time, though, our first home journey was wrought with a fair amount of stress. We first decided to build a home. This didn't go well. The builder wound up having problems and getting sued. And we were panicked—we had a baby on the way and nowhere to go!

We decided our next step was to work with an agent for a resale home in Lewisville, Texas. With the time crunch of my pregnancy, we looked at only a couple of places. As soon as we walked into 929 Hawthorne Court, we knew we had found the perfect place to raise our family. It was a gut reaction, but we both knew this home was where we were supposed to live. It was a two-story brick house with tall ceilings, parquet flooring, and an open floor plan. The backyard was huge and the perfect place for the large swing set we would eventually put there. Priced at $135,000, it was more than we wanted to spend at the time, so we had to get creative to come up with money for the down payment. But this house was meant to be for us, and a week after we moved in, I gave birth to our daughter, Caroline.

Our first home is the source of so many special and irreplaceable family memories. I brought both of my children home from the hospital to 929 Hawthorne Court. We celebrated their first birthdays there. I remember my grandmother taking a rare flight from North Carolina to Texas to meet our children in our home and posing for a multigenerational picture with the women of my family. My father lived in Tulsa, Oklahoma, and had a mulberry tree in his yard that we loved. During one visit to our home, my stepmother gifted us a sapling from their tree and we planted it with our children in the backyard.

Over the years, it grew into a beautiful twenty-five-foot tree that still stands today. And although we moved to Austin when my daughter and son were eight and six, they still talk about the home. To this day, my daughter still reminisces about how much she loved her bedroom on Hawthorne Court.

Our first home is a representation of who we are. I loved that home, and I'm proud of it. It taught me the value of owning something and making it into something you love.

Teresa Metcalf is the executive administrator in the office of the CEO and has been with Keller Williams since 2005.

CHAPTER 10

ENJOY SERVICE FOR A LIFETIME

When you were getting started on your home-buying adventure, you carefully selected an agent who values professionalism and who builds their business on stable relationships. Over the past few weeks or months, you've probably spent a lot of time together and gotten to know each other pretty well. There's no reason to throw all that trust and rapport out the window just because the deal has closed. In fact, your agent *wants* you to keep in touch.

"We tell buyers that we want to be the person they go to for everything," says agent Janet Faulk in Mooresville, North Carolina. "We have a wealth of information about homes and homeownership, and we want to continue to share that with our buyers, no matter how long it's been since closing." Agents call this commitment "service for a lifetime," and it's especially useful in that first exciting (and surprising) year of owning your home.

The reality is that a new home can be just as foreign as what's under your car hood. If you aren't well versed in the mechanics of either—you're going to be lost when something goes awry. But, like a mechanic, your agent is an *expert* in what they do. "I like being with someone or having the advice of someone whose expertise is home buying," says new homeowner Carnell Roberts. "They're able to provide more knowledge about the process." Just because you've moved in, it doesn't mean that you can't continue to call on their expertise. After all, agents have to deal with contractors, mortgage brokers, painters, decorators—and about a million other people whose sole job is home care and maintenance. So, if you've loved the service you've received from your agent, don't hesitate to turn to them for future assistance.

In fact, some agents have even created what they've called "concierge" services for their clients. This service includes a number you can call or text that functions as a directory and will provide you with an entire suite of information, from who to talk to about decorating a kitchen to who to hire to install a new bathtub. For a new homeowner with no experience, this kind of information can be invaluable. "We have kept in touch with our agent," notes Austin homeowner Erika Winders. "We consider her a friend now and continue to get her advice on the real estate market as we consider future home purchases."

You also may be surprised by how much you learn in the weeks and months after closing. There are all those things, such as a lawnmower or drill, that you probably didn't think about needing. There's that first maintenance emergency—a hassle, but you'll get through it. There may even be surprises in your own life, such as an unexpected pregnancy that suddenly makes your perfect two-bedroom one-bath home feel a little too cozy. Or a thrilling new job opportunity that changes your carefully chosen commute route.

Whatever surprises your life holds, your agent will be happy to provide expertise and advice. You, too, can prepare for many surprises by becoming knowledgeable about your home's systems, quirks, and needs. To help you, we've filled this last section with helpful tips, tricks, and strategies to help you get through that first year of homeownership like a pro!

Start Smart: Home Investments with the Best ROI

One of the best things anyone can do in their first year of homeownership is small home improvement projects that will instantly add value to their home. With some thought and a little sweat equity, you can tackle projects that not only make your house feel more like your own, but also will pay back dividends down the line. We've spoken with agents and narrowed down some of the top home improvement projects any new homeowner can tackle.

1. Add a Little Curb Appeal

One of the best ways you can take your starter home to the next level is by creating a little curb appeal. From creating that pergola in your garden to mulching the flowerbeds, there's a plethora of ways you can turn the outdoors into an extension of your living space.

But, if you've been living in an apartment or renting a home, you may not have all the tools required to help you in your task.

First things first, make a list of all the tools you think you might need, and start doing some digging around to find out what will work best for your plans and your home. From shovels to lawnmowers to gardening gloves and pruning shears—there may be a lot of new purchases to be made. But with a few new or borrowed tools and some elbow grease, you can take your new house and make it a showstopper.

"Plants can take years to grow, and if you want large plants, they are expensive. So, you can usually get away with smaller plants to start out. If you plant them right after you move in, then they'll be mature when you need to sell. I do that first for my own homes. Plus, then I get to enjoy it." **—Julie & Ed Huck**

"Outside, think nice borders around outdoor features, planters, water features, and color. Pavers are a great way to add some design and sophistication to an outdoor area. There are many floral options for just about every climate and every season. They will help beautify the area and attract pollinators. Once you create your design, make sure you won't hit any public utilities if you have to do any serious digging. After you're finished, don't forget to add the mulch. Mulching is a final touch that will make everything look great!" **—Sam Hasty**

"Plant trees the second you buy a house. A one-hundred-dollar tree becomes a tree that could cost thousands of dollars to replace. Plant ten trees or more, and you've made your home more desirable and potentially worth more." **—Gary Keller**

2. Refresh Your Look with Quick, Easy Fixes

One of the easiest and most affordable ways to freshen up a room and make it your own is paint. Paint can transform a room, give a space life, and make dingy walls look bright again. All that's required is a bucket of paint, some brushes, and a weekend with your partner or friends. There is a myriad of quick, inexpensive fixes you can make to give your home an instant facelift—even before you move in: scraping popcorn ceilings, installing new carpets, or even putting in a new countertop.

"One of the easiest and most cost-effective improvements is paint! Keep in mind that neutrals appeal to the most people, thereby making your home accessible to more people once you decide to sell. A gallon of paint generally costs less than twenty-five dollars." **—Wendy Papasan**

"Something I've seen lately is people doing wood treatments on accent walls. It's really easy to do, and if you're even a little bit handy (you don't even have to be very handy), you can choose a simple geometric design and achieve the same results. It looks really nice, and it's inexpensive. I had a guy do it for a house he was flipping. I think it cost them $300 to do the dining room wall, and it put a very refined finishing touch on it. It may not increase ROI, but it gives the house a very polished feel." —**Danny Charbel**

3. Tackle the Heavy Hitters

There are some home repairs that need to be done but are more time or money intensive. From new air-conditioning units to a new roof, sometimes larger things just need to be updated. After all, even if you plan on turning around and selling five years down the line, you'll get more out of your home with a new heater or back porch. And you'll get to spend five years enjoying your house instead of complaining about how cold the house is in the winter.

"Typically, first-time home buyers are in their mid to late twenties and don't have a lot of disposable income after they buy their home. The temptation is to turn their house into a 'HGTV house' as soon as possible. The reality is that they should prioritize how they upgrade their house into three categories: must-haves (mechanical, electrical, plumbing, roof), nice-to-haves (flooring, upgraded kitchen, upgraded bathrooms), and money in reserve for incidentals." —**James Williams**

"I advise clients, once they buy their home, to try and set aside five thousand dollars for emergencies. Most heating systems will cost you five to six thousand dollars, and they'll be most of the way there should they need a new roof. I try to set them up to be financially comfortable when those expenses come up." **—David Monsour**

"Number one: buy a home warranty. An HVAC unit or other old systems can be quite costly, so home warranty is not, and in most cases, the home warranty will cover that and therefore greatly reduce the financial risk of buying a property with old systems. So, I'm a big proponent of home warranties to reduce that potential cash outlay after six months in your new home." **—Brandon Green**

"There are a lot of homes I'll go into with a buyer and say, 'Unless you plan on being here for five years or longer, doing these updates won't get your money back right away.' But if anybody tells me that they're looking to stay in the house long term, I try to advise them on what to buy and update to keep a low investment in the home but still keep it really hot." **—Charles Tamou**

4. Find Those Perfect Fixtures

There are little touches that can elevate any space, from a new ceiling fan to updated drawer pulls. Lighting can be just as transformative as a coat of paint. No one likes a dark, dingy room—especially one lit by unappealing brass wall sconces from a bygone era. So, if you feel like you're living in a cave or are haunted by archaic ceiling fans, consider adding a window or new light fixture to create more light and a more modern look.

"An easy upgrade to your new home would be updated light fixtures. It is an easy way to update the look of the home and make it feel like yours. This is an inexpensive way to increase the value of your home over time." —**Jen Davis**

"If the house lacks light, consider adding skylights above the stairway or owner's bathroom to increase the natural light."
—**Anna Kilinski**

"Kitchen and bathroom hardware, light fixtures, new faucets, or even installing a new luxury shower head in the main bathroom are great, inexpensive ways to update a property."
—**Shaina Moats**

"When you're updating light fixtures, you have to be solving one of two problems, either you're updating the style, or you have a deficiency (such as there's a closet that doesn't have light). What I wouldn't do is overspend on things like light fixtures. Ceiling fans are a perfect example—you can buy a ceiling fan for forty dollars, or you can buy a ceiling fan for nine hundred." —**Nick Waldner**

Keep a List of Projects

If you're struggling to try and figure out which projects to tackle first, agent Charlotte Savoy offers some sound advice: "Keep an ongoing list of big and small things that you'd like to do around the house. It helps you budget and stay focused on the goals that you have to improve the house. And, when you do have an extra bit of money, you can do the small things like swap out light fixtures or doorknobs to something more modern. Little things go a long way!"

Try to budget around long-term remodeling plans, and only select one or two major projects to tackle a year. Maybe this first year, you'll paint all of the rooms, plant some trees, and buy a new light fixture for the front entry. Pick and choose your projects as you go, budget, and you'll have an amazing house full of memories before you know it.

5. Make Savvy Upgrades and Save Money

Another great option is to find ways to upgrade your home and pocket some cash. This could mean investing in newer, energy-efficient appliances or putting in a rain barrel so you don't need to hike up the water bill to keep your garden green. The great thing about many of the different ways you can upgrade your home is that they're often smart financial choices. Take new windows, for instance. While the price for purchasing and installation may be a larger chunk of change, the amount you'll save on your heating or cooling bill with energy-efficient windows can be a huge boon.

"There are many great ways you can invest in your home and improve its value, like painting or adding a security system. A home-energy audit is also a great way to save money." **—Brad Davis**

"I love things like the Nest thermostat or any smart thermostat to manage costs and energy usage when you are home and to make adjustments remotely." **—Sarita Dua**

"For homeowners who want to make their homes more green, even the smallest changes can make a difference in the long run. Changing lightbulbs to LED is an eco-friendly change that is relatively inexpensive and can have a lasting impact on your electricity bill. Installing a programmable thermostat is another way to make your home more efficient and save on electricity." **—Lance Loken**

6. Make Extra Mortgage Payments

One of the best things you can do in the first year of living in your new home has nothing to do with hammers or yard equipment—it's making extra payments on your home. In fact, extra payments are a smart call whether it's your first or fiftieth house. Moreover, as a new homeowner, if you put less money down, making extra payments can cut off years' worth of interest and get you out of your PMI faster.

"Budget to pay extra mortgage payments every year. My husband and I make an extra payment every month, but even one extra payment a year can cut years off your mortgage interest!" —**Sarah Reynolds**

"I recommend everyone make their mortgage payments bi-weekly, and if their lender allows, weekly payments are even better. The amount is the same, but you're paying the principal down faster, and with fifty-two weeks versus twelve months, you end up naturally making extra payments without ever feeling it or even thinking about it." —**Troy Williams**

"If you get a thirty-year mortgage, the likelihood of you staying there thirty years, well, is pretty slim. You can always pay more, but you are not obligated to do so. Paying just one extra mortgage payment a year could reduce the term of your loan significantly. You may not have tons of extra income, but if you get something unexpectedly, consider paying your note down. Or just budget by paying a little extra each month! That can go a long way." —**Anna Kilinski**

Onward

Buying your first home is a challenge and a joy. Like most firsts, it comes with a multitude of unknowns. But those unknowns are where our lives are lived and our stories are made. The camaraderie with our partners over a home improvement task accomplished. Laughter when we try to fix the sink, only to douse ourselves in water. Children running through rooms, once empty, now full of toys and laughter. Friends enjoying a slice of pizza as a thanks-for-helping-us-move token as you grab the last pack of boxes from your apartment.

It's these moments that make a house a home and these moments that make life worthwhile. We hope this book helps you in your journey to just such a life, one lived in the comforting four walls of your new home. We hope it has functioned as a guide and a source of comfort when you thought you couldn't possibly tour another house or sign another piece of paper. We have all had these same trials and tribulations, these same firsts, and we've look forward to helping you find your own. Here's to your first home, your last home, and all the memories in between.

Onward!

APPENDIX

Your Agent, Your Team

KEEPING TRACK OF WHO DOES WHAT

When it comes to buying a house, you aren't just working with one person. In fact, in a lot of cases you'll end up working with an entire team of people. If you find yourself scratching your head trying to figure out who is who, this worksheet will help you keep track of everyone's name and information.

Your Agent

Email

Phone

Other

This can be a loan officer, mortgage broker, or mortgage banker

Lender

Email

Phone

Other

Inspector

Email

Phone

Other

Contractor

Email

Phone

Other

Seller's Agent

Email

Phone

Other

Appraiser

Email

Phone

Other

Closing Agent

Email

Phone

Other

Insurance

Email

Phone

Other

NOTES:

The Right Home: Wants and Needs

WRITE YOUR WANTS

Figuring out what we need starts with knowing what we want.
In the space below, list all of your home wants. This can be anything from flooring
preferences and location, to the number of bedrooms you'd prefer.

_____
_____
_____
_____
_____
_____
_____
_____
_____

WHAT TO WHY

Examine the list above. What's the why behind your wants? Take a few minutes to
figure out the underlying values that support your wants, and write them out below.

Values:

DIVIDE IT UP

Based on your values and what you feel you need, divvy
up your wants into short-term and future needs.

Immediate:

_____
_____
_____
_____
_____
_____
_____

Future:

_____
_____
_____
_____
_____
_____
_____

GLOSSARY

Actual Cash Value: a type of homeowner's insurance policy. It's typically a less expensive form of coverage that only reimburses you for the cash value of what was lost or damaged, minus depreciation.

Adjustable-Rate Mortgage: (often referred to as "ARM"), as the name suggests, these have interest rates that fluctuate—or adjust—over the life of the loan. Unlike their fixed rate counterparts, whatever interest rate you secure at the time is only temporary.

Contractual Addendums: an attachment to a contract that modifies its original terms and conditions.

All-Peril (insurance policy): an insurance policy related to homeowner's insurance. It covers damage from anything not specifically excluded in the policy language.

The Americans with Disabilities Act: Passed in the 1990s, the Americans with Disabilities Act (ADA) prohibits discrimination on the basis of disability. This includes discrimination in employment, governance, accommodations, commercial facilities, transportation, and more.

Amortization: the process by which your lender calculates all the interest you will pay over the life of the loan, plus the amount you are borrowing, and divides that by the total number of payments you'll make.

Annual Insurance Premium: the annual payment made to an insurance company in order to keep that policy active.

Appreciation: the increase in something's value over time. In the case of a home, it's the increase in your home's value, which is generally determined by the local real estate market as well as any upgrades made to the home.

Appraiser: a professional who determines the market value of an asset.

Assumption: the conveyance of an existing mortgage to a new purchaser. This usually includes the terms and balances of the original mortgage.

Bankers: an employee or owner of a bank or group of banks.

Buyer's Agent: a type of real estate agent that specializes in buyers.

Buyer Representation Agreement: an agreement signed by a buyer and their agent that states that any home purchased will be bought with the help of that agent for an agreed-upon period of time (namely, the time with which you agree to work with that agent).

Canadian Real Estate Association (CREA): a certified trade association that represents real estate professionals in Canada.

Capital Gains Tax: a tax levied on sold assets. It's a tax based on the growth of the value of the asset at the point at which it is sold.

Character: the kind of homes, streets, and parks that a given area has to offer.

Closing Costs: sometimes referred to as settlement costs, closing costs are the fees associated with closing on your loan. They can include the lender's own fees, third-party fees for requirements such as title insurance, and the cost of prepaying a year's worth of property insurance.

Competitive Market Analysis (CMA): an analysis your agent will put together when you're searching for a home. It includes a set of MLS records about recently sold homes that resemble the one you want in size, condition, location, and amenities. See "comps."

Collateral: an item or property pledged by a borrower to protect the interests of the lender.

Commission: a fee paid to an agent or participating party for their role in a transaction or overall service.

Comparables (comps): The recently sold homes that resemble what you're looking for in a home. Part of a CMA. See "Competitive Market Analysis."

Condominiums: a building or complex in which apartments or townhomes are individually owned by their residents.

Contractual Disclosures: any documents a party is contractually required to disclose.

Covenants, Conditions, and Restrictions (CC&Rs): rules or codes that govern a piece of real estate. CC&Rs are a common practice among HOAs. See "homeowners association."

Deductible Rates: a deductible is the amount of money you must pay toward something that is insured. It's either a fixed dollar amount or a percentage rate. Most homeowner's insurance policies are percentage deductibles, and the rates are calculated based on the insured value of your home.

Down Payment: a percentage of the purchasing price of your home that you pay out of pocket.

Easement: a part of the property that can be used by another, nonowner entity. For example, a utility easement may exist so a cable company can access any wires or other cables buried on the property.

Encumbrances: claims against a property, such as a lien. Encumbrances can impede the transfer of title.

Equity: the portion of your home's value that you actually own. That is, it's the money that would go into your pocket after you sold it, paid off your mortgage, and handled any selling expenses.

Errors and Omission Insurance (E&O): insurance that protects you from lawsuits due to mistakes made in professional service.

Escrow: a separate, third-party account that holds a percentage of the money for a transaction before it is finalized.

Escrow Officer: the person responsible for real estate transaction processing.

Fair Housing Act: a law that prohibits housing discrimination based on race, gender, sex, disability, familial status, national origin, and more.

Fiduciary: a professional who acts with the clients' best interests front-of-mind, rather than their personal profit.

Fixed-Rate Loans: mortgage loans where the interest rate you pay is secured or "fixed."

Home Warranty: a type of warranty that helps cover the cost of minor home repairs or systems replacements.

Homeowner's Association (HOA): an organization that governs rules and regulations for a subdivision, planned community, or condominium. They have the authority to levy fines on homeowners who don't comply with community regulations or standards. Most are funded by fees collected from residents.

House-Hacking: when a buyer purchases a piece of real estate—a single family home or duplex—and lease out one of the bedrooms or units to help cover costs.

Insurance Assessor: sometimes referred to as an insurance adjuster. Someone who investigates claims to determine how much an insurance company should pay for damages.

Interest: a fee charged at a particular rate that is paid toward a lending institution on top of the principal sum that is borrowed.

Lien: a claim against an asset that is used as collateral in the case of a loan or debt.

Mortgage Broker: someone whose job it is to know and find the best lenders in the market.

Mortgage Interest Rate: the percentage of interest attached to your mortgage loan payments. Depending on the loan, this rate will either be fixed or adjustable. See "Fixed-Rate" and "Adjustable-Rate" mortgages.

Mortgage Officer: loan officer. The person who evaluates and authorizes a loan application.

Mortgage Payment: the amount of money you pay toward your mortgage loan every month. Your mortgage payments are calculated based on your down payment, interest rate, and loan amount.

Multiple Listing Service (MLS): a private service for real estate professionals. An MLS is an organization that offers cooperation and compensation among brokers.

National Association of Realtors ® (NAR): an organization of real estate brokers. It's a trade association for those in the industry in the United States.

Net Worth: a measure of wealth. Put simply it's the dollar amount you get when you add up everything of value you own and subtract everything you currently owe.

Owner Financing: a form of creative financing when the seller actually holds the mortgage for you while you make payments.

Personal Property Insurance: insurance that specifically covers things that you own (e.g., things that are inside of your domicile).

Piggyback Loan: a loan that covers the difference between the cash you have and the cash you need to hit the magical 20 percent mark. For example, if you only have 10 percent to put down, you could take out what's known as an "80/10/10": an 80 percent first loan, a 10 percent second loan, and a 10 percent down payment. Used to avoid PMI. See "Private Mortgage Insurance."

Principal: the principal sum of the loan. In other words, the original amount borrowed.

Private Mortgage Insurance (PMI): a type of mortgage insurance required for conventional loans whose borrowers make down payments of less than 20 percent. See "down payment."

Property Taxes: a tax levied by the government that is based on the current estimated value of your property.

Property Inspector: someone who evaluates properties for compliance with modern safety regulations. Used to help make sure a house is insurable and what types of repairs the home may require.

PMI: See "Mortgage Insurance."

Replacement Cost Insurance: a form of homeowner's insurance. While generally more expensive, it offers more coverage than Actual Cash Value insurance. See "Actual Cash Value Insurance." Generally, it will pay to rebuild your entire home as it was before an event, should your property be destroyed.

Rent to Own: a lease option in which you lease the property from the seller until you have the equity or cash to buy it.

Seller's Agent: a real estate agent who specializes in working with sellers.

Seller's Disclosure: a written statement of the owners' knowledge of the property's current condition.

Tax Deduction: a tax incentive that reduces taxable income through noting things such as additional expenses.

Terms: the agreed-upon rules between two parties in a legal contract.

Title: the legal rights to a piece of property.

Title Insurance: a type of insurance designed to protect homeowners and lenders from financial loss due to imperfect or problematic title transfers.

Title Researcher: a professional whose job is to determine who has legal title for a piece of property.

The Truth in Lending Act: a federal law that protects borrowers from predatory or unfair credit practices.

Umbrella Policy: an insurance policy that protects you from liability on or off your property and can cover things beyond just your home.

Underwriter: member of a financial organization that assesses and assumes risk for other parties during transactions for a fee.

ACKNOWLEDGMENTS

An incredible number of people across the United States and Canada shared their thoughts, time, and wisdom with us during the research and writing of this book. We would like to thank the following individuals for their collaborative spirits and generosity:

Thanks to Dave Jenks, original coauthor and long-standing part of the Keller Williams family, for all of his incredible work on the original edition of *Your First Home* and for providing more wonderful insights and stories for the second edition. Writer Madelaine Davis did a fabulous job researching and updating this second edition from the strong work of the first edition team, Rachel Proctor May and Jolynn Rogers. Vickie Lukachik also contributed her research and writing talents to the first-home experiences of our Keller Williams leaders. AprilJo Murphy's editing advice and expertise brought this second edition to fruition.

This book wouldn't be able to hold the hands of its readers and walk them through the home-buying process without the tremendous amount of insight the following individuals offered to us: Lysi Bishop, Elizabeth Campbell, Danny Charbel, Dianna Clark, Robert Colello,

Amy Cromer, Jen Davis, Sarita Dua, Mike Duley, Thomas Elrod, April Florczyk, Tricia Gray, Brandon Green, Sam Hasty, Alex Helton, Adam Hergenrother, Dan Holt, Julie and Ed Huck, David Huffaker, Julia Lashay Israel, Kevin Kelly, Anna Kilinski, Lance Loken, Michelle Madding, Christine Marchesiello, Erin McCormick, Kymber Lovett-Menkiti and Bo Menkiti, Kimberlee Meserve, Shaina Moats, David Monsour, Shawn Morrison, Wendy Papasan, Lesley and Andy Peters, Dakoda Reece, Jim Reitzel, Jeff Reitzel, Sarah Reynolds, Shiloh Sadoti, Brady Sandahl, Charlotte Savoy, Kayla Smith, Josh Stern, Charles Tamou, Sandi Terenzi, Nick Waldner, Hallie Warner, James Williams, and Troy Williams.

You can't buy a home without having your finances in order. Thank you to these financial professionals who took time away from their work in order to help our second edition readers take the first step to greater net worth through homeownership: Zander Blunt, David Eckert, Barbara Frierson, Monica Jenkins, Leslie Linder, George Milligan, and Jeff Reitzel.

First homes hold a special space in our heart. Our thanks go out to the homeowners who shared their experiences with us for this second edition: Melissa and Kevin Ankin, Pat Bauer, Valerie Blakey, Debbi Cohen, Amy Gilbert, Holly Gorman, Amy and Brian Katz, Erica and Dave Mass, Lynda McDonald, Carnell Roberts, Melissa Robertson, Becky and Matt Sirpis, and Erika Winders. We remain grateful for the homeowners who told their stories for the original edition.

Part of what we believe makes this book so special are the homeownership memories it brings to life. We are indebted to Gary Gentry, JP Lewis, Linda and Jimmy McKissack, Teresa Metcalf, Althea Osborn, and Bill Soteroff for reminiscing with us. Their first-time home stories, as well as those from Mo Anderson, Sharon Gibbons, and Jay and Gary personify the wonderful, yet intangible aspects of owning a home.

Once a book is written, the work isn't complete. We were lucky to be able to collect feedback from some very smart individuals to help make this book shine. Our stellar reviewers include the following people: Zander Blunt, Mark Brenneman, Todd Butzer, David Eckert, Darryl Frost, Steven Hanlon, Tami Jackson, Garrett Lenderman, Kathleen Manchin, Jeff Reitzel, Bill Soteroff, and James Williams. Kyle Romero and Allison Turner helped us infuse just the right humor into the pages. Cindy Curtis designed a beautiful book that we are proud to display on our shelves. Thanks to Caitlin McIntosh and Owen Gibbs for their help executing the vision.

We remain grateful for all the real estate and financial advice that was shared by the individuals in the first edition. We remain indebted to other contributors, who helped in a multitude of ways from offering advice to providing photographs that helped bring the first edition to market. We'd like to thank Ashley Reis for helping us snag a last-minute photograph just before deadline.

Thank you to our publishing partner Todd Sattersten at Bard Press for all his guidance in bringing this second edition to fruition. This second edition would not be on bookshelves today if not for the help of many of our peers. Kathryn Cardin, Ruben Gonzalez, Mindy Hager, Garrett Lenderman, Elise Poston, and Diane Tyler contributed their wit and support to us in the days and months we spent on this project.

It's the people that make a house a home, and it is this community that helped us quite literally make this book. Thank you, all.

INDEX

GARY KELLER

Gary Keller is cofounder and executive chairman of Keller Williams Realty. His *New York Times* bestselling books, including *The Millionaire Real Estate Agent* and *The ONE Thing*, have sold millions of copies worldwide, garnered more than 500 appearances on national bestseller lists, and been translated into nearly 40 different languages.

Gary graduated from Baylor University in 1979 with a degree in marketing and real estate. By age 26, he was the vice president of expansion for Austin's then-largest real estate company. Three years later, he resigned from the position and struck out to create his own real estate firm. Gary soon took his company and his philosophy of "people helping people" nationally, then internationally.

A noted philanthropist and supporter of the arts, Keller and his wife, Mary, live in Austin, Texas.

JAY PAPASAN

Jay Papasan is a bestselling author who serves as the vice president of strategic content for Keller Williams Realty, the world's largest real estate company. He is also cofounder of KellerINK and co-owner, alongside his wife, Wendy, of Papasan Properties Group with Keller Williams Realty in Austin, Texas.

Jay was born and raised in Memphis, Tennessee. After attending the University of Memphis, he spent several years working in Paris. He later graduated from New York University's graduate writing program and began his publishing career at HarperCollins Publishers. There, he helped piece together bestselling books such as *Body for Life* by Bill Phillips and *Go for the Goal* by Mia Hamm.

ALSO BY GARY KELLER
AND JAY PAPASAN

THE ONE THING

The ONE Thing is a book for busy people. It will teach you that the results you get are directly influenced by the way you work and the choices you make. You'll learn how to identify the lies that block your success and the thieves that steal time from your day. By focusing on your ONE Thing, you can accomplish more by doing less. Join over two million other readers who have found extraordinary results from asking:

What's your ONE Thing?

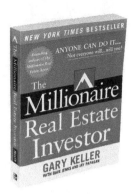

THE MILLIONAIRE
REAL ESTATE INVESTOR

Once you start reaping the benefits of your first home, you'll understand the enormous economic opportunity that real estate presents. *The Millionaire Real Estate Investor* is a how-to guide that reveals the models, strategies, and fundamental truths millionaires use to become wealthy through real estate. But the *New York Times* bestseller isn't just about real estate. It also takes a hard look at the money myths that hold some people back from financial freedom and the money truths that let others soar.

THE MILLIONAIRE REAL ESTATE AGENT

This national bestseller begs the most important question anyone in real estate sales could ever ask: How do I take my sales income to the highest level possible? Believe it or not, it is a simple question with a simple answer. The *Millionaire Real Estate Agent* lays the how-to groundwork for you to think like a "Millionaire Agent." The book will show you, step-by-step, how to earn and net a million in annual income—active and passive.

CPSIA information can be obtained
at www.ICGtesting.com
Printed in the USA
JSHW081651071122
32739JS00008B/8